D0927947

PARACHUTES AND PARACHUTING

PARACHUTES

AND PARA

by Bud Sellick

CHUTING
A MODERN GUIDE TO THE SPORT

Prentice-Hall, Inc., Englewood Cliffs, N.J.

Parachutes and Parachuting: A Modern Guide to the Sport by Bud Sellick
Copyright © 1971 by Prentice-Hall, Inc.
ISBN 0–13–648535–9
Library of Congress Catalog Card Number: 75–153950
Printed in the United States of America T
Prentice-Hall International, Inc., London
Prentice-Hall of Australia, Pty. Ltd., Sydney
Prentice-Hall of Canada, Ltd., Toronto
Prentice-Hall of India Private Ltd., New Delhi
Prentice-Hall of Japan, Inc., Tokyo

Dedicated to Scott and Tanya

PEANUTS ®   By Charles M. Schulz

Ten years ago, when I wrote *Skydiving,* parachuting as a sport was just an infant. The parachutes used then were essentially the same as those used by Leslie Irvin to make the world's first free fall in 1919.

To those of us who cut our teeth on non-steerable, flat circular canopies, the revolutionary blank-gore, sleeve-deployed modification presented a whole new aspect to the sport. Today the sport parachute is designed and constructed with high-performance capabilities undreamed of ten years ago. Several paraglider designs are now available, for example, that are not "jumped," but rather "flown." Controls for steering and breaking allow speeds up to 30 mph horizontally, yet featherlight touchdown landings at two to five feet per second. When we refer to "experienced" jumpers today, we are talking in the range of 300 to 500 delayed free falls on steerable canopies. Where ten years ago we could buy a surplus canopy for $15 and work it over with pinking shears to come up with a sport canopy, today you aren't likely to purchase anything new for less than $300 or so.

And techniques have changed considerably in the past decade.

Ten years ago, when two or three jumpers maneuvered together to pass a baton or hold hands in free fall, everybody marvelled. We now have accomplished twenty-man stars, caterpillars, diamonds, and lines-abreast relative-work formations.

Ten years ago Dick Fortenberry made the first dead-center landing in a world's championship competition. In 1970, at the Tenth World Parachuting Championships in Bled, Yugoslavia, Don Rice of the U.S.A. won the gold medal and world accuracy champion title with three dead-center landings and one of twelve centimeters. A Russian trailed by two centimeters with three dead-centers and a fourteen centimeter jump. A decade ago a style jump consisting of an international series (two figure-eights and two backloops) was quite an accomplishment for most jumpers. The 1970 style champions accomplished this feat in less than eight seconds.

With such drastic advances being made during the past decade, both in equipment and in skills, I took the task of writing an up-to-date book about parachutes and parachuting. Frequently, by the time I had received all the data and supplementary photographs from one individual or manufacturer, another would present me with more current information on another aspect. After several years of rewriting, revising and updating, I have at last acknowledged the fact that technology in the field of parachuting is accelerating more swiftly than writers can write, and publishers can publish, a book. At this time, this is the way it is.

So many people have assisted in the writing of this book that I wish I could acknowledge everyone—that in itself would account for a major part of this work. The cooperation of Norm Heaton and the United States Parachute Association has been invaluable. Lyle Cameron, editor and publisher of *Sky Diver Magazine,* furnished information, materials, and support. Among the photographers who furnished me with hundreds of negatives and prints, special thanks go to Ralph White, Joe Gonzales, Carl Boenish, and the late Bob Buquor. Others, working with the manufacturers and developers of specialized equipment, are Ed Drumheller of Irvin, Ed Vickery of Pioneer, Chuck Embury of Parachutes Incorporated, and Steve Snyder of Steve Snyder Enterprises. For their editorial help, a very special thanks to Dan Poynter and Pierce Ellis.

Bud Sellick
Nashville, Tennessee

CONTENTS

PARACHUTES AND PARACHUTING

Leonardo da Vinci sketched this parachute design in 1495. Although never actually constructed, there is every reason to believe it would have worked.

1

HOW IT ALL BEGAN
Our Parachuting Heritage

The term *parachute* comes from two root words: *para* which means *shelter* or *guard against,* and *chute* which means *fall.* Any device that slows a falling object so it lands safely can be considered a parachute.

The *Mona Lisa* of the parachuting world is illustrated here. Three years after a fellow Italian discovered America, Leonardo da Vinci did this sketch for his *Codex Atlanticus.* Although the force of air was recognized in ancient times and was used to push sailing vessels, Da Vinci was one of the earliest to conceive the idea of air supporting a man's weight. He sketched and made notes about a glider; several flying machines that had flapping wings and relied on muscle power; the retractable landing gear to cut down on drag; a flying saucer with movable wings that resembled oars; an air-screw of the helicopter design; and the parachute pictured here. Of the parachute, he wrote, "If a man have a tent of closely woven linen without any apertures, twelve braccia across and twelve in depth, he can throw himself down from any great height without injury."

The size of Da Vinci's chute is determined by his unit of measure—a *braccio*. The term comes from the Italian word meaning "arm." It is defined as an arm's length by some sources and, by others, with figures ranging from fifteen to thirty-nine inches. One source nails it down to exactly 18.4 inches. Using these extremes, his chute was anywhere from fifteen feet square to thirty-nine feet square. I don't know about you, but my arm measures twenty-nine inches, and a twenty-nine-foot square pyramid holds approximately the same volume of air as the standard parachute used today.

Some sources credit Fausto Veranzio, a hundred years after Da Vinci's sketch was published, with designing and actually jumping his parachute. While it is true that Veranzio drew a picture of a square canvas parachute being used from a tower, there is little evidence to support his claim that he actually jumped with it. In those times (1595), the designer usually gathered a huge crowd around him to watch his initial attempt at anything as dramatic as this, since the first attempt was frequently the last attempt.

Other names crop up in various history sources as possibly being the first to make a parachute jump. Joseph Montgolfier, the balloonist and paper maker, claimed to have parachuted from the top of his home in Annonay, France. Sebastien Lenormand, professor of technology at the Paris Conservatory of Arts and Handicrafts, claimed to have parachuted from the Montpelier observatory. In 1785, Jean Pierre Blanchard, the balloonist, experienced difficulty with his over-inflated balloon over Ghent and is credited by some sources as being the first to jump from a balloon. He claimed he broke his leg on that emergency jump and, if he actually made the jump, he also deserves a special notice as receiving the first parachuting injury.

Finally, in 1797, balloonist André Jacques Garnerin made the first of many undisputed exhibition parachute jumps from his balloon. His first was over Paris with thousands watching.

Garnerin's parachute was made of silk with a supporting pole and looked like a huge reinforced umbrella. Standing in a basket at the end of the pole, he released his chute and then oscillated violently as the unvented canopy spilled air first from one side and then from the other. He apparently was sticking to Da Vinci's instructions that the material should be "without any aperatures." One source says this first jump was from 8,000 feet, while another says it was from 2,000 feet. Those of us who have jumped the flat circular chutes sympathize with him and hope his jump was from only 2,000 feet.

Sir George Cayley proposed an inverted cone to eliminate objectionable oscillation. He claimed to have built such a chute and that a German, Lorenze Hengler, safely descended from as high as 400 feet on several occasions. Cayley's idea for eliminating oscillation also may be credited with eliminating the first parachutist. The first known parachute fatality took place in 1837 when Robert Cocking took a 5,000-foot plunge in his collapsed, cone-shaped chute. The French astronomer, Joseph Lalande is given credit for eliminating a great deal of this oscillation when he suggested a hole in the top to allow a small portion of air to escape, making the canopy more stable. Almost thirty years later, the American Captain Thomas Baldwin also advocated the vent in the apex claiming it helped in slipping or guiding his parachute as well as providing stability.

Until the balloon, there was little opportunity to use a parachute. Ironically, the parachute was used almost exclusively for exhibitions. Although the early balloons were made of treated paper and lifted by the heat of burning straw, the idea of using a parachute for emergencies never came to light. Because parachuting had always been thought of as a stunt, the first life-saving jump in 1808 was a novelty. Jodaki Kuparento parachuted from his burning balloon over Warsaw. His method of exit and operation of the parachute is unknown.

Normally, before the balloon ascended, the apex of the parachute was attached to the bottom of the balloon's gondola. Strung out beneath the balloon as it ascended were the balloon's gondola, the parachute canopy and lines, and the parachutist in his basket. At the proper height, the balloon's pilot would cut the line that secured the canopy to his ship. The balloon would shoot up and the parachute would drift down.

Jumpers soon found the crowds less enthusiastic when it became apparent the parachute would lower them safely. Exhibition jumpers needed a gimmick. Removing the parachute basket, they substituted a trapeze bar and did all manner of unsafe and insane stunts as the balloon ascended and as the parachute descended. This helped, but soon the crowds wanted more.

By the early twentieth century, even the trapeze bar was becoming passé. Then, somebody struck upon the idea of hiding the parachute in a sack and riding up without displaying it to the crowd. The surprise of seeing the man drop free of the balloon for a moment was enough to bring some of the crowds back.

The sack with the parachute folded inside was secured to the balloon's basket. A break cord was attached to the apex of the parachute and to the basket. When the jumper released his trapeze, he would drop, breaking the cord on the sack and allowing lines and canopy to be drawn out. When the chute was completely extended, his weight would break the cord that held the apex of his chute to the basket and he would float free. Since there was now the question of the canopy catching air and inflating, the crowds watched each drop with bloodthirsty anticipation. The hot-air balloon and the parachutist on the trapeze bar became standard items at county fairs, circuses, and other crowd-gathering events through the late 1920's. A few of those daredevils lived to become highly respected sport parachutists. Charles E. Dame, now president of the New Hampshire Parachute Club, and a United States Parachute Association Area Safety Officer, is pictured on page 15. His cotton parachute is folded neatly above his trapeze as he descends beneath the hot-air balloon.

Meanwhile, back at the ranch . . .

While balloons and parachutists continued to cavort around the sky thrilling crowds, others were working very seriously on the idea of a heavier-than-air machine that would actually fly.

Sir George Cayley, who designed the inverted-cone parachute to reduce oscillation, earned the title "father of British aeronautics" for other reasons. Fifty-five years before Lenoir completed his first practicable gasoline engine, Cayley had proposed an airplane, propeller-driven by an engine. The problem of flight, he stated, was "to make a surface support a given weight by the application of power to the resistance of air." He constructed a biwinged glider and incorporated into it his theories of initial velocity, wing loads, bending movements, lightness, and strength. He designed it to be as streamlined as possible, using a revolutionary cambered wing—a basic necessity for lift—rather than a flat surface. His biplane was constructed soundly with struts and diagonal bracing, and fitted with horizontal and vertical stabilizers. It flew with a hired hand aboard in 1809—almost a hundred years before the Wright brothers' first powered flight.

Orville and Wilbur Wright had scientifically built gliders, tested them in their own laboratories and their own wind tunnel, but gliders had been developed—powered flight had not. Experimenting in powered flight, Otto Lilienthal and Percy Pilcher had killed themselves in crashes. Penniless and frustrated, Alphonse Penaud had committed suicide at the brink of success. Clement Ader, Sir Hiram Maim, and Dr. Samuel Langley had spent many thousands of dollars and the pooled knowledge of the world's greatest aeronautical minds and had failed. The Wright brothers succeeded, however, and powered flight opened new realms for the parachute.

In 1909, the powered airplane was solidly (for that day anyhow) in the aviation picture. The Wright brothers were now regularly flying as much as an hour or more. Glenn Curtiss had built his first plane and was flying it. Glenn Martin had also built a plane and was flying it. Louis Bleriot had flown across the English Channel.

To help finance his aviation enterprises, Glenn Martin staged a demonstration in 1910 and charged spectators to watch him fly his contraption. The demonstration was so successful, he continued to make exhibition flights and charge for them. By 1913, he had discovered that simply keeping his plane aloft was no longer thrilling the people. He needed a gimmick—just as the balloonists a hundred or more years before him had. His gimmick was the parachute. For bonus points, he added sex Miss Georgia "Tiny" Broadwick, teen-age veteran of many drops from hot-air balloons, became the first woman to parachute from an airplane—his Martin hydroplane. Martin built a trap seat alongside the fuselage and rigged the parachute so a static line would open the chute after Tiny slid from her perch.

A year earlier, over Venice, California, Grant Morton had made the first parachute jump from a plane in flight. Carrying the chute folded in his arms, he threw it into the air as he leaped into space. The pilot, Phil Parmalee, was considered to be the one recklessly taking chances, since it was then believed that the sudden loss of the parachutist's weight would throw the plane hopelessly out of control.

That same year, near St. Louis, Captain Albert Berry made the first jump from a plane using the pack-type parachute. The parachute was stowed in a metal container attached to the plane's skid, with a rope extending up to a belt worn by Berry. He climbed down to the axle and at an altitude of 1,500 feet and a speed of 50 mph, dropped away, drawing the parachute from the metal container as he fell. The plane was a Benoist pusher biplane piloted by Anthony Jannus. Here, too, the pilot was taking the chances; but Tony Jannus had already made a name for himself as a daring pilot when he flew a Benoist flying boat 1,970 miles from Omaha to New Orleans—in only thirty-nine days!

When World War I came and the military took over the airplane, it somehow neglected to take over the parachute—after all, the parachute was still nothing more than a stuntman's tool. There was little thought of a pilot trusting his life to such a thing when he had the security of his sturdy flying machine. During the war, hundreds of balloonists acting as artillery spotters and observers had their balloons shot down and saved themselves by parachute. Parachutes were okay for balloons and observers, but no respectable pilot would be caught dead with one—and sure enough, none were.

When the chivalry of the aviation fraternity fell apart and enemy pilots began shooting at each other instead of waving, some great pilots died because they were without chutes. Some apparently considered it cowardly to wear a parachute, feeling that bailing out of a plane was dishonorable. The German pilots didn't think so and began wearing static-line-operated Heineke sack-type parachutes, similar to those used in jumping from balloons. In 1916, an Austrian pilot on the Russian front successfully bailed out after his plane was shot to rags. A few weeks later, another Austrian pilot saved his life by bailing out. From that time on, all German and Austrian pilots wore parachutes. The British, French, and Americans were still reluctant to use a parachute and many leaped from flaming planes, preferring to die in the fatal plunge than burn in the falling wreckage. Just as the war ended, a few Allied pilots began to carry parachutes in their planes.

The war had stimulated aviation more in those few years than all the aeronautical geniuses of the world had been able to do since the dawn of history. The successful use of the parachute during the last stages of the war convinced the United States government that a reliable parachute needed to be developed.

In 1918, a board was set up by the U.S. government to begin development of a parachute that would meet the following requirements:

1. It must be possible for the aviator to leave the aircraft regardless of the position it might be in when disabled.

2. The operating means must not depend on the aviator falling from the aircraft [as the static-line-operated parachutes did].

3. The parachute equipment must be fastened to the body of the aviator at all times while in the aircraft [the chute was stowed in a bag in the plane and a strap with hook was fastened to the jumper who pulled the chute after him as he fell].

4. The operating means must not be complicated or liable to foul, and it must not be susceptible to damage through any ordinary service conditions.

5. The parachute must be of such size and so disposed as to give maximum comfort to the wearer and permit him to leave the aircraft with the least difficulty or delay.

6. The parachute must open promptly and must be capable of withstanding the shock incurred by a 200-pound load falling at a speed of 300 miles per hour.

7. The parachute must be steerable to a reasonable degree.

8. The harness must be comfortable and very strong and designed so as to transfer the shock of opening in such a manner as to prevent physical injury to the aviator. It must also be sufficiently adjustable to fit the largest and smallest person.

9. The harness must be so designed that it will prevent the aviator from falling out when the parachute opens, regardless of his position in the air, and at the same time it must be possible to remove the harness when landing in the water or in a high wind.

10. The strength "follow through" must be uniform from the harness to the top of the parachute—bearing in mind the old axiom— "No chain is stronger than its weakest link."

11. The parachute must be so designed that it is easily repacked with little time and labor.

All these conditions sound fairly rigid even by today's standards. Remember, though, these conditions were being made when only a static-type parachute was in use and then usually from a balloon or slow moving airplane.

The board included such men as Major E. L. Hoffman, Guy M. Ball, Ralph Bottriel, J. J. Higgins, A. Leo Stevens, Floyd Smith, Glenn Martin, J. M. Russell, and Leslie Irvin. They tested every known parachute of that time, foreign and domestic, and none would qualify. Leo Stevens and Glenn Martin had worked earlier with Charles Broadwick in developing an attached-type parachute that could be worn by the jumper and activated by a static line. Stevens had actually suggested a free-fall type parachute which would be manually operated, as early as 1908. Most parachutes, however, had remained in a sack attached to the balloon or plane. The jumper fell away with nothing but a belt hooked to a strap leading up to the suspension lines.

Only a parachute that could be worn on the jumper and activated manually at a safe distance from the disabled plane could be accepted. Static lines and sack-type developments would easily tangle with the falling craft and drag the parachutist down with it.

A free-fall parachute had one big catch to it—almost everybody still believed that the air would be sucked from the jumper's body as he fell and he would be unconscious or dead within seconds. Pilots may have fabricated this myth during the war to comfort themselves after seeing a fellow aviator leap to his death to escape a flaming plane.

Leslie "Sky-Hi" Irvin didn't believe this. As a parachutist he had dropped more than two hundred times using the static-line arrangement from balloons and planes and had never felt a loss of breath during the brief plunge before the chute completely inflated. He had also performed in a circus, high diving eighty feet into a net, with no difficulty breathing. These two reasons were enough to convince him that he would not die simply from falling free of the plane. There was still another reason he didn't believe the unconsciousness theory. During his earlier parachuting days, he saw a parachutist fall to his death. Irvin was standing only yards away from the point of fatal impact and had seen the man flailing his arms and legs right to the moment of contact. "Sky-Hi" reasoned that, if a man can wave his arms and legs all the way to the ground, he must be conscious and therefore able to activate a parachute. Irvin may have been the first to conclude that it isn't the fall that hurts, it's the sudden stop.

Yet there was still another problem. Many people still felt that a man in space, even if conscious, would be little more than a helpless glob, unable to effectively control his movements without a firm footing for leverage. Based on his own body control during high dives into the net, Irvin was convinced he could maintain control of his movements as well as remain conscious. To prove it, he volunteered to make the world's first free-fall jump.

On April 28, 1919, Leslie Irvin buckled on the model A, manually-operated parachute and climbed into a De Havilland DH-9 biplane at McCook Field near Dayton, Ohio. At the controls was Floyd Smith. In telling of this dramatic moment in his life, Irvin said it wasn't until he stood up in the cockpit, 1,500 feet over McCook Field, that he found himself rapidly losing confidence in his ability to stay conscious, control his movements, and activate the parachute. He didn't hesitate any longer, dived headfirst over the side, delayed only a few seconds, then easily pulled the ripcord with both hands. The parachute blossomed perfectly and an exuberant Irvin descended. Although he broke his ankle when he struck the ground, he said he smiled all the way to the hospital!

He had reason to smile. Not only was he still alive, but he had proved—or disproved—several points about free-falling bodies. He demonstrated that it is possible for a man falling through space to remain conscious, think, and make coordinated movements to manually release a parachute.

Irvin was one of our earliest test jumpers. Although making a jump-and-pull hardly sounds daring to the present-day sport jumper, it was extremely so in Irvin's day—or at least everybody thought so. He faced the same enemy in 1919 that man has faced since the dawn of time and still faces today—the unknown. Man's instinctive fear of the unknown is as basic as his instinctive fear of falling—and the test jumper must overcome both. The parachuting world lost a great man when Irvin passed away in 1966.

During the 1920's, aviation boomed and Irvin built a parachute factory and his parachutes saw plenty of action. While Major Hoffman's group began working on the next great problem—delayed free fall—flying circuses barnstormed the country. Surplus airplanes from World War I were easy to buy —still "in the manufacturer's container" as we say today. Men like Charles A. Lindbergh and James H. Doolittle bought their planes in a box, assembled them on the spot, and flew them away. Some flew away to fame and fortune, some just flew away, and some never got off the ground.

After barnstorming the country, first as a parachutist and then as a flyer, Lindbergh took up flying the mail. And although he had saved his life by parachute four times—twice in the military, twice flying the mail—he made his historic Atlantic flight without one. Jimmy Doolittle also saved himself with a parachute on four separate occasions. His fourth jump was at night over China after his historic B-25 raid on Tokyo. Others on that mission bailed out—one died jumping, several were killed or captured by the Japanese, and the rest made it back to become heroes. One accidently opened his chute in the plane, repacked it, finished just as the engine ran out of fuel, and then safely bailed out!

In 1922, Lieutenant Harold R. Harris (who retired as a general) made the first emergency jump from a disabled plane and saved his life with an Irvin parachute. Less than a month later, Lieutenant Frank Tyndall became the second man to jump from a disabled plane and save his life with an Irvin

Chute. Shortly after this, several members of Irvin's parachute section suggested making some sort of club of those who saved their lives by parachute and the Caterpillar Club was born. Harris and Tyndall became the first two members, both military pilots, although earlier, William O'Connor had saved himself with an Irvin reserve when his Jahn chute failed.

The list of names from the Irving Air Chute Caterpillar Club files reads like a *Who's Who in Aviation*. By 1935, the club had a membership of more than 1,000 grateful airmen . . . and airwomen like Mrs. Irene McFarland. She saved her life over Cincinnati on July 4, 1925—a month after Lindbergh's second emergency jump. By the end of World War II, Irvin's parachutes had saved more than 80,000 lives. Thrilling stories of many of these jumps are related in Ian Mackersey's book, *Into the Silk*.

During the 1920's, planes were continuously being improved to go higher and faster. High speed emergency bailouts were inevitable and the parachute test section went to work on the problems of delayed free fall. Men like Randall Bose and Steven Budreau bailed out at altitudes up to 7,000 feet to experience the first encounters with the deadly flat spin. The delayed fall was necessary to allow the pilot's body to slow down for the parachute opening.

From tests, it was discovered that the free-falling human body accelerates up to 120 mph and then, in a flat position, falls no faster. This speed is referred to as "terminal velocity" and might be compared to the sonic barrier for airplanes. Terminal velocity is reached in approximately twelve seconds, after the drop of roughly 1,500 feet. The test jumpers experienced very little difficulty up to terminal velocity, but delays past 1,500 feet brought on various peculiar forces, especially the tendency to rotate. This turning would be relatively slow at first and, depending on the movement of the body, would rapidly accelerate until everything became a blur or it would stop and counter-rotate. There seemed to be a constant battle to maintain a heading. More jumpers like Crawford, Morgan, and Whitby made delays, sometimes fighting off the spin, sometimes resorting to the ripcord before losing consciousness. Free-fall testing reached a climax in August, 1960, when Captain

Joseph W. Kittinger stepped into space at 102,800 feet. He had fallen sixteen seconds and reached a speed of 614 mph when a six-foot stabilizing chute automatically deployed to prevent spinning during the next four and a half minutes of fall before his main chute automatically opened. He tells his story in his book, *The Long, Lonely Leap.*

While the military test parachute group was cautiously and scientifically tackling the problems of delayed free fall from 8,000 feet, civilians like Art Starnes and Spud Manning were making exhibition delays from as high as 18,000 feet.

The barnstormers and their flying circuses were in the public eye. Scientific test jumpers were not. As a result, the parachute kept its image as a stuntman's gimmick—just as in the days of balloons. To the general public, the parachute was strictly for daredevils who liked to flirt with death or for aviators who had no choice. Unfortunately, this same general feeling exists even today.

Parachute jumps were a necessary part of any airshow, as much as the airplane itself, but because people could watch the show from the surrounding countryside, the air circus people had to get down near the ground and put on some stunts that only the paying customer could see—those right at the field, not half a mile away. This is when the shows began smashing automobiles head on into each other, doing car-to-plane transfers, and wingwalking. Art Starnes had a leather pad sewn in his thick canvas pants and would drop from a plane a few feet off the ground, scooting along in a cloud of dust with his famous seat-of-the-pants death-defying slide. Everybody within miles could see his parachute jump, but only the paying customer saw that "slide of death" act. Somehow, though, the parachute was associated with the same absurd stunt.

This reminds me of another parachutist, Buddy (Emmett L.) Plunkett, who should have had Art's leather-bottomed pants for a stunt he did at Daytona Beach. He was making a car-to-plane transfer. Standing on a roadster and facing backward as it roared down the beach, he waited for the Jenny to overtake them. The first pass was too fast and Plunkett signaled the pilot to slow down. The second pass was slow enough but too high and he missed it. The pilot thought he was still too fast so slowed down even more for the third pass. Plunkett had no difficulty grabbing a wing-skid and swinging his legs up around it. His weight on the wingtip plus the slow airspeed caused the plane to dip, then skim along the sand with Plunkett hanging on for dear life. He bounced along, seat first, a la Starnes, but sans padding. After his rear had been sanded sufficiently, it was treated to a soothing (ouch!) saltwater bath as the pilot turned out to sea in an effort to gain altitude. Plunkett still hung on for dear life, his raw rear slapping the tops off waves as he went.

Starting out as a wingwalker for Mabel Cody's Flying Circus in Atlanta, the fourteen-year-old Plunkett immediately took to parachutes and thrilled crowds all over the entire southeastern states with his daring stunts both with and without a parachute. He became known for his long delayed free falls—one from 23,000 down to 9,000 feet—and repeated "malfunctions." Actually he carried an old torn chute, let it trail a few thousand feet, and would then open his main. Without a doubt, his most spectacular and death-defying parachute jump came over Tampa Bay when he soaked his plane with gasoline and ignited it! He secured a can of gasoline to the top wing of the old biplane and then ran copper tubing down and out along the leading edges of the port and starboard lower wing to each wingtip. He put a valve under the can and punched holes in the copper tubing. On each wingtip he installed a spark plug, wired to a booster magneto in the cockpit. The idea was to release the gasoline along the wings, ignite it, and as the plane was slowly consumed by flames, bail out. It worked pretty well up to the point where he released his seat belt and cranked the magneto. Apparently the gasoline had not just trickled back along the lower wing but had been picked up in the propblast and whipped up onto the bottom of the upper wing and the sides of the fuselage, too. When the spark ignited the gasoline, the entire plane exploded into flames instantly. Plunkett dived over the side and delayed his opening long enough to watch the plane arch over in a ball of flame and dive toward the Gulf of Mexico. He opened his chute and settled gently into Tampa Bay where a boat was waiting and recovered him. The nineteen-year-old collected a nifty $1,200 for the stunt.

During the 1930's parachuting saw another gimmick come into play—bat wings. Even today the bat wings are used occasionally. Outlawed by The United States Parachute Association, bat wings have seldom been used for much more than display purposes. The typical bat-winged jumper would walk around in front of the crowds, swooping his canvas and stick contraption up and down, demonstrating how he would be using it in flight. It made a good show on the ground—and still does for that matter—the crowds loved it. But in the air, that's a horse of another color. With few exceptions, the bat-winged parachutist would plummet like a crated piano, usually trailing a sack of flour to mark his trail as he fell.

There seems little doubt that the majority of the exhibition jumpers using bat wings look pretty sick compared to skilled skydivers who glide without wings. The maximum track demonstration by Ed Deluca and Al Solis of the U.S. Army Parachute Team is enough to convince most people that skilled skydivers *do* move in some direction other than straight down. The display of bat wings isn't necessary when you see two men leave the plane together at 13,500 feet and open up nearly four miles apart! Who needs bat wings?

In all fairness to birdlovers, exhibitionists with bat wings deserve some credit for carving their own spot in the parachuting world. Many of them carved their own spot in the ground as well. Most left a lasting impression.

Clem Sohn killed himself through carelessness in Vincennes, France, on April 25, 1937, when his parachute fouled in the bat wings. He had successfully demonstrated his wings a couple times in Miami. One account reported that, "Leaping from a plane only 3,000 feet up over Portsmouth Airport, Hants, England, Clem Sohn swooped like a bird for a mile, then parachuted into a tree." He wore a standard backpack and used a seatpack for an emergency chute, leaving his chest free of obstructions for a better glide. His bat wings consisted of treated canvas over metal rods strapped to his arms, waist, and legs, and another piece of canvas fixed between his legs. His last jump was from 10,000 feet and he supposedly glided down to within 700 feet of the ground before pulling his main.

Charles Dame of Rochester, N. H., rides a trapeze aloft under a hot air balloon in 1927. His parachutes are stowed in a sack over his head. On this particular drop, he made a triple drop, cutting away from the first and second chutes to alight with the third one—a thrilling show even by modern standards.

Leslie L. Irvin descends on Mc-Cook Field near Dayton, Ohio, in 1919 after making the first free-fall parachute jump in history. (*Irving Air Chute Co.*)

Leslie L. Irvin, ca. 1927-28. The parachuting world lost a great man when Irvin passed away in 1966. (*Irving Air Chute Co.*)

Barnstormers mixed wingwalking and ground-to-air transfers with the parachuting and stunt flying—giving parachuting the daredevil connotation it still has. Here Buddy Plunkett re-enacts some of his wingwalking routine.

In the late 1920's, Emmett L. "Buddy" Plunkett (center) thrilled thousands with his barnstorming acts. He survived to become a colonel in the Air Force. Colonel Plunkett owned and operated a certified parachute loft near Atlanta, Georgia. He died in 1971.

By the time the CAA came into being and issued a ruling that required exhibition parachutists to wear two parachutes, Buddy Plunkett already had over a hundred jumps with only one. Here he proudly displays his dual rig.

Fifty years before this photo was taken, free fall was thought to be suicide. It was believed a person would be unable to breathe, air would be sucked from his lungs, and unconsciousness and death would result. Even if he could remain conscious, they said, with nothing to brace against, movement would be impossible. (*Bob Buquor*)

For those unfortunate enough to have descended under the old standard 24-foot emergency canopies—non-steerable, unstable, and fast-descending—the obvious conclusion was that it saved lives the hard way. Security Parachute Co. came up with this angel of mercy: a low porosity, steerable, 26-foot conical reserve chute. (*Security Parachute Co.*)

The Barish Sailwing, introduced in late 1965, is ancestor of a number of designs that have reached the sport parachuting market. Although it produced the outstanding forward speed desirable, opening shock and opening reliability presented problems. Dependent on forward speed for its lift, it stalled like an airplane at slow speeds and dropped like a rock. (*Jerry Irwin*)

oneer's Volplane, a ram air
rachute, being introduced by
ary Patmor at the U.S. National
rachuting Championships in
70.

Batwings are more valuable for showmanship on the ground than gliding through the air. Pictured here are Tommy Boyd, Don Molitar, and Lyle Cameron. (Sky Diver Magazine)

Irvin Industries and Steve Snyder pooled efforts to come up with the Delta II Parawing. The slotted wing and improved deployment system put this design out in front of the solid deltawing designs. (*U.S. Navy*)

Security's Cross-Bow came on the market in 1964 at the same time that Pioneer released the Para-Commander. For a while jumpers sided with the P-C or with the Xbo, but it was a short-lived battle. With accuracy being measured in centimeters, the Xbo dropped into second place. (*Jim Pol*)

Astronaut Ed White spent 21 minutes in space outside Gemini IV—which ranks among the longest "free falls" in history. Like a free-falling skydiver, White was also falling and having similar sensations of weightlessness. But unlike the free-falling jumper who uses air to turn and maneuver his body, White used a hand-held self-maneuvering unit. (*NASA*)

Pioneer's Para-Commander revolutionized sport jumping in 1964. Although many others offer plus features, the P-C (or sister designs) is currently the most common and most accepted sport parachute in the entire world. (*U.S. Navy*)

Steve Snyder flys his Para-Plane, a ram-inflated paraglider that looks more like a flying mattress than a parachute.

The pilot chute caught in a wing preventing the canopy from inflating. He then pulled his reserve seatpack at 250 feet, but it fouled in the other malfunction and he was killed on impact.

Another 1937 report tells of Manos Morgan who started his jump from 10,000 feet and glided for ninety seconds before opening his parachute at 1,400 feet, landing safely. Without wings, he would have covered the distance in fifty-three seconds. His wings were three-and-a-half feet across and were made of steel tubing with airplane fabric.

Tommy Boyd, like Sohn, wore a seatpack for his reserve when using bat wings. Unlike Sohn, Boyd was still alive at last accounting and his glide was said to approach thirty to forty degrees (forty-five degrees is considered tops in maximum track without wings). Tommy filled his leg fin with red powder and pinned it shut with clothespins. When he jumped, a static line pulled the pins, allowing him to trail the dust down to the opening at four or five hundred feet. This low opening might account for the optimum glide ratio since the lower the opening, the greater the illusion of distance traveled.

Although his wings apparently had nothing to do with it, Rudolf Boehlen of Switzerland died of internal head bleeding the day after three successful flights. He is thought to have struck his head during a backward parachute landing fall.

At last report, bat-winged jumper Red Grant decided wings were too dangerous and lived to retire.

Probably the most well known of the winged jumpers was Leo Valentin. He died with his wings on in 1956 when the propblast from his jump plane smashed one wing against the door and he hurtled to his death. Valentin deserves credit for being more than the rest, although he ended up just as dead. He was the first to perfect delayed free-fall techniques. He dreamed of someday accomplishing flight without using the parachute—actually landing with his wings. He had several close calls early in his career with various types of non-rigid wings and after a particularly harrowing experience in 1950, concluded that this type of wing could do little more than slow the free fall. It became obvious to him, he said, that it was impossible to glide with non-rigid wings.

He scientifically designed a set of rigid wings some nine-feet-long with a hinged arrangement on a steel tube corset for his chest. As he was about to test the twenty-eight-pound rig from a helicopter he later stated, "I have rarely felt so hideously insecure." Leo was a master of understatement. The wings were stressed to lock up against a support so they could be folded forward but not back—this was necessary to keep the wings from folding behind him and breaking both arms. He was right, it worked perfectly as he began his drop from 4,000 feet. Suddenly he was flipped on his back where the wings closed together with a slam—and he began the horrible, panic-stricken ride down, spinning on his back, struggling to free his arms of the wings so he could pull the ripcord. He never figured how he did it, but the ripcord was pulled at 900 feet. He lowered his corset and wings to the ground on a rigging line. His friends and fellow batmen, Salvador Canarrozzo and Soro Rinaldi congratulated him for surviving. Salvador, who developed the arrow-like inverted "Y" position of stable free fall, was to die in 1953 when his one and only chute failed at 450 feet.

In his book, *Bird Man,* Valentin tells of watching his two friends perform. After watching these bat-winged companions jump with flapping canvas wings, Valentin realized he needed more than mere surface, if he were to glide successfully. He designed rigid wings with a true airfoil and took flying lessons to better understand the art of flying and gliding.

Valentin's final set of wings were of balsa wood, weighed twenty-eight pounds, and had a locking system that once opened, held them open with no danger of collapse. He had tested his "tail"—canvas stretched between the legs in one large solid section—and discovered it caused spinning, so this was eliminated. After testing his new wooden wings in a wind tunnel—first on a dummy, and then on himself—he made his first jump with them on May 3, 1954, becoming the first birdman to truly fly, covering more than three miles from 9,000 feet on the first attempt.

Because Valentin made his living as a professional parachutist, he became billed as "Valentin, the Most Daring Man in the World." He had no objection to this billing, since it produced his living, but he said it was only a constant warning to him to practice prudence at all times. He found himself making a jump with canvas wings in order to fulfill a contract, but observed, ". . . it was painful for me to be forced, in order to satisfy a press and public more eager for sensations than for quality and research, to go on with a stunt which I knew led nowhere." Leo kept carefully within the safety limits (1,000 feet for the opening is France's safety limit—six seconds above the ground) and shuddered at the recklessness of his fellow birdmen. He said he was neither a madman nor an eccentric. To him, parachuting was a serious business and he carefully packed his chutes, carefully checked his instruments, always opened within safe limits. He was not the first to point out that the risk is great enough when a pure accident is still possible. Valentin was highly critical of Salvador Canarrozo whom he called both a wonderful pal and a most daring parachutist. Canarrozo always jumped without helmet, goggles, watch or altimeter, or a reserve parachute. He would judge his own time for pulling the ripcord, usually no higher than 500 feet ("When a Ford looks like a Ford," as my good friend Johnny Findley likes to put it). The reckless Italian birdman made his last impression at Venice in April, 1953. The safety conscious, careful, prudent Valentin died in May, three years later.

While exhibitionists were wingwalking or making midair plane transfers or otherwise displaying more guts than skill, pilots were competing in air races. It was traditional at air races to supplement the show with a demonstration parachute jump or two. A fee of one hundred dollars or so would be paid the jumper and that would pretty much be the end of that until the next year's races. Sometimes the jumper would land in front of the people and sometimes he would float halfway to Timbuktu —these were non-steerable parachutes. Steerable sport parachutes were still twenty years away. To get a top-notch jumper who could always land at least on the airport, (don't laugh) the fee would be higher—up to five hundred dollars for some jumpers.

One jumper, back in 1926, suggested to the Pulitzer Races authorities that instead of hiring one man to jump at their Philadelphia show, why not put the money up as a prize and invite several jumpers to compete for it? This way, the show would get more jumpers, better jumpers, and still pay no more than for one. The idea sounded good to jumpers and sponsors alike and the jumper who had suggested it, Joe Crane, became the father of competition jumping. This wasn't sport, though —that's for glory—this was strictly professional, winner take all. A circle was made on the field and the jumper whose average was closest to this spot became the winner and walked off with a cash prize. The others walked off with experience. This "spot jumping" contest became a popular event in future airshows and at the National Air Races.

The race was held each year and the number of jumpers increased. By 1932, forty-six contestants were signed to compete. Up to then, the jumps were unsupervised and every man was independent of all factors except himself. Crane was placed in complete charge of the jumpers during the two-day air meet at Roosevelt Field in the fall of 1932. He organized the group and scheduled the jumps so that instead of the confusion of previous races, the jump program came off smoothly, each jumper knew exactly what he was to do. Although jumping had been incidental to the air races, it began to have a place of its own now. The National Aeronautics Association had not been interested in the jumpers, but only the pilots. However, NAA's Bill Enyart recognized parachuting as a vital drawing card for the races and formed a parachute committee with Joe Crane as president. A few months later, a group of professional jumpers met at Roosevelt Field and formed the National Parachute Jumpers Association. As an organization, they quoted minimum charges for air meets. During the '30's, Crane maintained records and sent out periodic newsletters to the more than a hundred members. By the time the World War II broke out, NPJA had 250 members. Although continuing to work closely with NAA at the air races, Crane and his jumpers' association maintained their independence.

During this same period—the late 1920's and early 1930's—a Russian military attaché visiting the United States was impressed with the parachuting practices of the Americans. He and his military leaders realized the potential military advantage of trained parachutists and took the idea back to Russia in 1925. Stalin himself ordered jump schools for the training of boys and girls as well as adults. The next year, the American parachutist Lyman Ford made the first free-fall parachute jump ever made in Russia. (Thirty years later, as president of Pioneer Parachute Company, Ford furnished the first U.S. parachute team with the chutes they used in Moscow during the Third World Parachuting Championships.) In 1927, the Russians demonstrated how nine paratroopers could parachute behind the lines and dynamite enemy installations. By 1932, trained military parachutists had reached a degree of proficiency that enabled them, during war games, to capture the entire "enemy" headquarters and all the Soviet officers in command of the opposing force.

The parachute turned up for sport jumping in 1930 for the first time when the Russians held a special sport festival that included a spot jumping contest. These were not professionals jumping for money, but civilian factory workers jumping for nothing more than fun or honors. In 1933, the year after NAA created a parachuting committee in the United States, the Soviet government grouped all Russian parachute clubs under one national organization.

With the government supporting the movement, sport parachuting engulfed Russia. By the mid-'30's, Russia was making mass drops of 5,700 military troops and had begun dropping light tanks and artillery pieces. Automatic openers were used by the Russian troops rather than static lines. In 1935, sport jumpers were training on 559 state-subsidized training towers at the 115 parachute centers. These same sport jumpers needed only military training to become expert paratroopers. By 1939, they became parachutists fighting in the Russo-Finnish wars—and winning.

While sport parachuting can be credited to the Russians in 1930 (regardless of their motive), seeing the military application of the parachute goes back to an American, Benjamin Franklin, who suggested the idea in 1784. In 1928, Billy Mitchell arranged for six soldiers to parachute from a bomber over Kelly Field, assemble a machine gun, and set up a defensive position in a matter of only minutes. He had suggested the idea ten years earlier during World War I. The ranking officers who witnessed the demonstration of airborne mobility and firepower enjoyed the show but failed to be impressed with the military significance. It wasn't until 1940 that William Ryder and William Lee led the original 48 volunteers through training to become the first American paratroopers.

Both the Germans and French *had been impressed* by the Russian paratroop exercises and both began to train their own military jumpers. The French, like the Russians, used free-fall parachutes. Unlike the Russians, the French allowed each man to pull his ripcord rather than having it pulled by an automatic opener. This meant that some opened their chutes immediately on exit and a few didn't open at all—the rest were straggled out in between, at the mercy of the winds and the sharpshooters below. This could account for the French more or less giving up their parachute troops, but becoming the leaders in the art of delayed free fall.

The Germans carefully weighed the evidence of the Russians and the French and developed the static line which put all troops open at the same altitude and kept them in one group rather than scattered all over the sky and countryside. In 1936, Raymond Quilter presented a static-line system for military troops, but the British War Office wasn't interested. The British, like the Americans, failed to see any real significance in parachute troops until *after* World War II broke out.

Then, in 1940, the Germans dropped storm troopers on Holland and took the city of Rotterdam entirely with airborne troops. The British and Americans suddenly saw the light and both immediately initiated crash programs. There was little reason why those German troop carriers couldn't have flown another few minutes and dumped German troops on Great Britain instead of Holland. That twenty-mile moat no longer gave the British the sense of security they had enjoyed earlier.

The weather in Great Britain often leaves much to be desired when it comes to flying or parachuting, so part of the training was done indoors. Moored balloons inside huge hangars were used as training towers. The jumper was released with his canopy already held open, just as American jump towers did. Night and day, rain or shine, training continued on a crash basis. After the indoor training, the British paratrooper made seven jumps—two from a moored balloon and five from an airplane—to receive his jump wings.

In the early days of parachute troop training, only the Americans wore reserves. Consequently, fatalities among the Russian, French, German, and British troops were more frequent. During early training, a fatal accident was considered a good thing as long as it happened to somebody else—the rest of the troops felt another fatal accident immediately after the first was unlikely and for the next few days the air would remain safe.

While Russia and Germany were using the parachute as a military weapon against their fellow man, parachute troops to fight fires began to train with the United States Government Forest Service. Although the idea had been tried in 1934 by a professional, J. B. Bruce, it was abandoned as too risky and efforts were concentrated on chemical bombing of fires. By 1939, it became obvious that the available planes could not do the job and Frank M. Derry was put in charge of a group of professional jumpers who would parachute in to fight fires. Early results showed that in only nine fires, the men had saved three times the cost of the entire project, earning a permanent slot in parachuting history. Over the past twenty-five years, smoke-jumpers have proved themselves to be invaluable, saving millions of dollars worth of valuable forests.

World War II saw the parachute expand in several fields—especially with airborne troops and aerial delivery of military equipment—but the most outstanding and exciting stories come from the emergency uses—airmen leaping for their lives. More than 100,000 persons saved their lives with parachutes during that war. Some, like British pilot Tony Woods-Scawen, saved themselves several times. Woods-Scawen was shot down five times, safely parachuted to earth the first four—the fifth escape was too low for the parachute to deploy and he was killed.

Others survived to greater glories. Colonel Charles E. Yeager is a good example. Early in his flying career the engine of his Bell Airacobra blew up and his cockpit filled with flames. The P-39 went into a powerdive and Yeager fought the flames and his safety harness at the same time. He fought his way clear, tumbling first, then gyrating wildly on his back as he pulled the ripcord. The high-speed opening shock knocked him unconscious. He woke up in a hospital where doctors told him he'd fly again—and did he ever!

Late in 1944, the day after he had shot down a German Me-109, a swarm of FW-190s raked his Mustang with cannon shells. The engine and oxygen system exploded into flames and his well-ventilated cockpit became a raging furnace. With shell fragments in his feet and a badly cut arm, Yeager dived into space 20,000 feet over enemy territory. To avoid hanging like a clay pigeon for the 20 minutes of descent, he delayed his opening for more than a minute, opening his parachute at 5,000 feet. Although enemy troops were all around him and he could hardly walk because of his wounds, he avoided capture and made his way back to England.

Those of us who know him can hardly imagine him ever being angry. But Chuck Yeager didn't like walking home and he got downright mad. His first mission out he shot down a

German bomber. On a mission a few days later, he shot down five German fighters, and a few weeks later, his propeller-driven Mustang shot down a new Messerschmitt Me-262 *jet* fighter. Two weeks later he blasted four more German fighters out of the sky. In a matter of a few months, the mild-mannered, quiet-talking West Virginian had twelve confirmed air-to-air kills. Yet today, Yeager is best known as the first man to fly faster than the speed of sound, pushing the old Bell XS-1 through the barrier in 1947. He hit 760.5 mph in level flight—then a few years later, more than doubled that speed to again set a world's record. He insists that it took no courage for him to bail out of his plane either time—that jumping out was so much better than staying inside, he probably would have done it without a parachute.

Thousands of exciting stories came from parachuting episodes during the war and many good books are filled with stranger-than-fiction accounts.

After the war, some of the returning military parachutists continued making jumps as civilians, just for fun. Some attempted long delays, panicked, and pulled the reserve instead of the main. Sometimes the rig was unsafe and the reserve would rip off on opening. Unfamiliar with the free-fall pack, the ex-paratrooper would fall to his death without attempting to open his main parachute. The Civil Aeronautics Board issued a regulation outlawing delayed free falls at airshows, but Joe Crane's NPJA expanded to take in certified riggers and became National Parachute Jumpers-Riggers, Inc., NPJR. He worked through the NAA to establish parachute records with the Federation Aeronautique Internationale. In 1948, the FAI set up an international parachuting commission and the NPJR affiliated with NAA. The commission set up rules for records and competitions, paving the way for the 1st World Parachuting Championship that was held in Yugoslavia in 1951. No Americans took part in the first championships—there were representatives from only five countries and the winner was Pierre Lard of France. When France hosted the Second World Parachuting Championships in 1954, the number of nations had increased to eight and Sergeant Fred Mason, competing as the only U.S. entry, finished twenty-first. The Russians won the event and so became host in Moscow in 1956. Between 1954 and 1956, NPJR members expressed some concern that the Americans had only one contestant rather than a team—Fred Mason looked pretty lonesome in those pictures that showed complete men and women teams for several countries.

One such concerned person was Jacques Istel who vowed to do something about it. He was a delegate to the Commission of International Parachuting Championship in 1955. While in Europe, he took time off in his native France (Istel is a naturalized American) where Sam Chasak and Michel Prik taught him the basics of controlled free fall. Istel came back and immediately went to work promoting an American team. He worked with the late Joe Crane and the NPJR, sent out invitations, and trained those who could participate. In 1956, he lead the first American team into world parachuting competition. From then on, the U.S. team grew in size and in prestige with Americans either winning or placing in the top positions.

When Istel began pushing the sport in 1956, interest began to grow among people other than professional jumpers or ex-paratroopers. College groups got together the next year for an inter-collegiate meet and clubs began to spring up across the country. By late 1957 the NPJR had changed names once more and became the Parachute Club of America, again with Joe Crane as president. The next year, Jacques Istel and Lewis B. Sanborn set up Parachutes Incorporated and devoted full time to sport parachute promotion. Shortly afterward, they opened the first commercial sport parachuting centers at Orange, Massachusetts, and at Hemet, California. In 1967, the Parachute Club of America again changed names and became the United States Parachute Association, with Norman Heaton remaining as executive director.

The late Joe Crane deserves a position of honor for giving birth to competition jumping and for keeping parachuting alive and organized for the first thirty years. Jacques Istel can be credited with giving birth to skydiving techniques and true sport parachuting in America. Istel is responsible for developing (in the U.S.) the sleeve and steerable sport chutes—two necessities if a jump is to be really fun. Those of us who started out with non-steerable, flat circular chutes, like to think those were the "good old days" when it took a real man to make a delayed free fall. When the ripcord was pulled you didn't count slowly to four while the sleeve deployed and your canopy swung you to a halt—you closed your eyes, gritted your teeth, and yanked. After the stars cleared and vision returned once more, you'd check to see how much canopy had been blown away—those holes weren't modifications then, they were honest-to-goodness holes. A few holes were good for cutting down the miserable seesaw oscillation that would rock you into urpy nausea. Then came the fun of trying to guess where you'd land.

British jumper Dumbo Willans said it and maybe we should call it Willans' Law: "There seems to be some kind of natural law by which parachutes generally avoid the really disastrous obstructions while taking every opportunity to land their 'pilots' in undignified and uncomfortable situations—sewage dumps, chicken farms, guard-dog compounds, grape arbours, tall trees, and church spires." I look back on these days of jumping in the same vein as my military experience—I wouldn't take a million dollars for the experience, but I wouldn't want to go through it again, either.

The sleeve for more positive and more gentle openings and the truly steerable canopies had a great deal to do with the growth of our sport and the reduction of injuries and fatalities. Istel introduced them both to popular usage in the United States. His limitless energy and personal drive pulled parachuting out of its doldrums and changed the attitude of many anti-parachuting officials.

The military, which had made free-fall parachuting a court-martial offense, reversed its decision and retained Istel to train a select group of military men in the art of free-fall parachuting. These seven men became the cadre of instructors for the Army. Early in 1958, AR 95-19 authorized army personnel to compete and take part in delayed free-fall parachuting. The other military forces later issued similar regulations. Istel had cracked the toughest opposition and turned the tide in his favor. He gave talks and demonstrations to state aviation officials who at first were anti-parachuting officials. The result was that those of us who were outlaw-jumping in defiance of state laws, could at last jump with state approval. Moreover, state approval opened the way for the formation of parachute clubs at various airports where invitations could be extended to interested spectators.

Convincing state officials of the safety of parachuting—when properly conducted—was one thing. Convincing the federal government was something else, though. In 1961, Istel had not only convinced the Federal Aviation Agency that parachuting should be recognized, he talked the FAA administrator, Najeeb Halaby, into making a sport jump at the Orange Sport Parachute Center. For good measure, Crocker Snow of the Massachusetts Aeronautics Commission came along and jumped, too. Talk about selling refrigerators to Eskimos . . .

In the fall of 1961, NAA asked FAI to send a list of the current world records on parachuting. Of the eighty-two world records, every one was held by an Iron Curtain country—Russia alone held sixty of them! Immediately, Istel and Sanborn, with two of their parachute center's instructors, Nate Pond and Bill Jolly, went to work to beat the Russians. In November, 1961, they broke the old Russian records and set new ones in the four-man team night-and-day group accuracy with delayed-opening category—the first of many U.S. entries in world parachuting records. By January, 1962, there were 124 world records on file with FAI. The two U.S. records and one new French record represented the entire free world. Later, in 1962, the U.S. began an all-out effort to capture more records. Within two years, the U.S. Army Parachute Team held seventy of them.

Meanwhile, the U.S. continued to enter parachute teams at the World Parachuting Championships. The U.S. had come in sixth out of ten in its first attempt in 1956; then, in 1958, in Czechoslovakia, it again placed sixth—but this time out of fourteen. In 1960, in Bulgaria, Barbara Gray and Sherrie Buck represented the women jumpers of America for the first time, but only as individuals, since four were required to make a team. At this, the Fifth World Parachuting Championship, the U.S. team placed fourth overall, but Jim Arender became the individual world style champion and Dick Fortenberry placed second overall, having scored the first dead-center ever recorded in world championship competition. We were on the move now and hosted the 1962 event at Orange, Massachusetts. This was the largest yet, consisting of twenty-six countries and 136 individual contestants. But on our home field we did the best yet. Jim Arender and Muriel Simbro took the overall World Champion title for men and women. Our men's team placed second to the Czechoslovakian team, but our girls took first place for the women. We repeated the performance in the 1964 world meet in West Germany when Dick Fortenberry and Tee Taylor took overall champion titles and our girls won first place for the women. The men's team dropped to third behind Czechoslovakia and Russia. The Eighth (1966) World Championships were scheduled for East Germany—a country not recognized by many of the western nations. As a result, the U.S. and several other nations did not take part. Since only six nations are required for the world championship, the game went on without us. The Ninth (1968) World Championships were held in Graz, Austria, where the U.S. team took first place. In 1970, the Tenth World Parachuting Championships were held in Bled, Yugoslavia.

We've covered a lot of ground—or should we say air—since Leonardo doodled his "tent" design. Special parachutes have been developed that range in size from a foot or so up to one hundred feet or more. The uses are endless—some will be discussed at length later in the book. Most developments in parachutes, like in aircraft, have come within the twentieth century. Special caliber men have risked their lives in developing the parachute and the related escape systems. From towers, balloons, and airplanes, for money, life, and honor, the parachutist today has a rich and exciting heritage.

2 THE PANIC BUTTON! Emergency Jumps

Emergency parachute jumps are the ones that seem most exciting (especially to the guy who makes one) and this type of parachuting is the most known to the general public.

The average person thinks of the parachute as that one link with life after all else is gone—the panic-type, last resort, emergency situation when all else has failed and there is nothing to lose by hitting the silk. This is the reason most people think of parachuting as death-defying and dangerous. They either associate it with some unfortunate pilot whose plane is burning and breaking up in flight where bailing out means little more than *how* he'll die, not *whether* he'll die, or they associate it with the barnstorming daredevil who risks life and limb flirting with death to thrill crowds and make money. The thought of bailing out of an airplane, even in an emergency, strikes terror in the average pilot. Half of the pilots you ask will tell you they'd rather ride down with the plane and take their chances on the crash than bail out. The majority seem to feel their chances are still better in a crash-landing than in a parachute jump. There are cases that justify either choice, but survival favors the man who bails out.

An emergency jump is exactly that—an emergency. This means you have only one parachute and if it doesn't work, there's little left to do except pray . . . fast. It also means you have no choice of when, where, or how you get away from the plane. It may be at night, it may be over a city, and the plane may be tumbling end over end or spinning. There are factors that are normally eliminated in a pre-planned jump such as a sport jump. For example, a sport jumper wears *two* parachutes; he chooses his own time of day and the right weather conditions; he usually jumps over open country or a prepared drop zone; and he exits a plane that is flying straight and level. There is little comparison between these two types of jumping, yet the average citizen groups them both in the same category—"a parachute jump."

Fate seems to play a big hand in the survival of airmen leaving their disabled aircraft. In March, 1964, George Neale, one of the Navy's Blue Angel precision pilots, plunged to his death when he ejected at 200 feet and his parachute failed to open fully. Yet in October, 1961, Navy pilot John T. Kryway ejected "on the deck," literally, from the carrier *Roosevelt* and survived with minor injuries. (An unusual sequence of photos was made by Louis J. Cera, USN, a very alert photographer who shot the dramatic event with a K-20 semi-automatic aerial camera.) And Navy Lieutenant Barry Kunkle survived with nothing worse than a broken leg when he ejected at flight-deck level from the carrier *Midway*.

But British Lt. B. Macfarlane takes the cake—starting at *below*-zero altitude. Macfarlane of the Royal Navy flew from the British aircraft carrier HMS *Albion* in October, 1954. His engine failed as he was catapulted from the deck. The plane struck the water in a nose-down attitude and began to sink. To top this off, the carrier then ran over the plane and shoved it down, broken in half, some twenty feet. At this point Macfarlane triggered his ejection system and blasted free of the wreckage where he released his straps and paddled to the surface with only minor injuries.

What must go down in parachuting and aviation history as that once-in-a-million event took place in March, 1963, over Frejorgue, France. A parachutist named Chionni stepped from the open cockpit of a small biplane to make a routine drop. Pilot Christian de la Beaume prepared to fly back to the field and land. Both were in for a terrifying surprise when Chionni's main parachute and harness struck the tail assembly and became hopelessly entangled. Chionni could not free himself and the plane was dragged to a stop, then began the plunge toward earth with the pilot still in the cockpit. The pilot cut the engine. Chionni went for broke and pulled his reserve chute. Both chutes inflated properly to check the descent. Although the plane was slightly damaged and the pilot suffered a broken leg, parachutist Chionni walked away unscratched. (*Paris Match*)

What's the lowest bailout? Lt. B. D. MacFarlane's plane lost power on takeoff from HMS *Albion,* hit the water and sank—then was run over by the ship. He was somewhere beneath the ship when he *ejected,* but eventually fought his way to the surface and survived. This sequence of ten photographs shows Lt. John T. Kryway ejecting at flight-deck level. His parachute opened in time to check his fall. A helicopter crew retrieved him moments later to discover he had suffered only minor injuries. Kryway was making a normal 130-knot approach to the carrier *Roosevelt* when rough seas caused the deck to dip slightly. The resulting rough landing caused the right wheel to break off and friction ignited the magnesium strut. Although the hook had caught the arresting cable, it broke under the strain and Kryway continued to hurtle down the deck toward a fiery finish. He quickly elected to eject—even at deck level—and survived to fly again. (*U.S. Navy*)

Emergencies develop in sport jumping, too. This unusual sequence of photos was taken by Soviet photographer-parachutist Gennadi Ikonnikov who was on the field making some routine shots of fellow jumpers loading up and exiting when an emergency developed 3,000 feet above him. Yuri Belenko had a malfunction, pulled his reserve which tangled with the main, and began the terrifying descent with a double malfunction. One of the jumpers on the ground looked up and saw the life-or-death struggle above. He yelled to fellow jumpers who grabbed a packing mat and began sprinting toward the impact point. Belenko continued to struggle to clear his malfunction while the men below stretched out the mat and waited. Belenko plummeted into the canvas at bone-crushing speed, ripping the tarp from the hands of his rescuers and knocking them to the ground. When the dust cleared, Belenko was gasping for breath and writhing in pain, but he was alive. Except for an injured leg and minor bruises and abrasions, he was none the worse for wear. At last report, he was not only walking again, but was planning another jump. These photos are stills taken from Ikonnikov's movie film. (Soviet Life *magazine*)

Emergency jumps are made when the emergency develops—
whether over trees, water, cities, or other hazardous areas. Tree
landings are rare in sport jumping now, although not before
steerable parachutes were developed. Usually the airman drops
through the tree safely while his canopy snares in the branches and
arrests his fall. A greater danger lies in getting down, out of the tree.
If the parachutist is wearing a reserve chute, he simply leaves it
attached to the harness and drops the canopy to the ground. Then he
carefully slips out of the harness and slides down the reserve lines
and canopy. Bud Kiesow made this tree landing for the filming of
the award-winning USAF training film, *Passport to Safety*. Parachuting Associates Dave Burt, Jim Hall, and Bob Sinclair also
participated in the production. (*Parachuting Associates, Inc.*)

And then there's the man who ejected at 1,000 feet, but whose chute didn't even come out of the backpack—and lived to tell about it. In February, 1964, Navy pilot Edward A. Dickson fell 1,000 feet, hit in a deep snow drift, bounced about 50 feet in the air, skidded along the snow, and slammed into a pine tree. Having never bailed out before, he assumed this was routine for an emergency ejection until he discovered his parachute still in the container on his back. His commander, flying another A-4 Skyhawk jet with him, circled overhead and saw Dickson's free fall and bounce. Making the best of the situation, Dickson pulled the ripcord on his chute to get the pack open, then wrapped himself in the parachute to keep warm while waiting for his rescue.

Some men just never give up. Navy Lieutenant Frank K. Ellis ejected from his Cougar jet only 75 feet over the ground near Point Mugu Naval Air Station, California on July 11, 1962. The story should logically end there, but it doesn't. His chute failed to open, and he crashed through a cluster of eucalyptus trees and into the ground—still in the ejection seat. His left leg was badly mangled, his right leg sheared off below the knee, his back broken, three ribs fractured, and his body covered with multiple burns, cuts, and bruises—but he was still alive. Two months later his remaining leg had to be amputated. He still wouldn't give in. Nine months later he was back at the controls of a T-33B jet taxiing around the field, trying out his two artificial legs and attempting to convince officials he was still capable of flying a plane. Double amputees just don't fly jet planes and the military, while admiring his spirit, said no. He decided to make a parachute jump to prove he could still perform as well as a man with two real legs. On May 19, 1963, he made a parachute jump at Gillespie Field with the San Diego Skydivers. That convinced the right people and, fourteen months after the accident, he was back in the air, flying a variety of aircraft. Frank Ellis became the only double amputee in the history of the Navy to continue on flying status.

Emergency parachute jumping goes back to Polish aeronaut Jordaki Kuparento's leap from his burning balloon over Warsaw in 1808. Even as late as 1919, two men saved their lives by bailing out of the blazing gondola of the *Wingfoot Express* over Chicago.

Emergency parachuting from airplanes starts with Harold Harris—the first man to be awarded the Caterpillar Club pin. Countless thousands have since saved their lives by bailing out.

Stories from Caterpillar Club files and other sources tell of incredible escapes in emergencies when there seemed no chance of survival. Flying Officer Rupert North dived from a Ventura with only a harness on and a QAC (Quick Attachable Chute) parachute in his hand. He snapped it on upside down (the left snap hooked into the right D-ring) by only one snap—then pulled. It worked.

John Vollmer didn't even snap his on at all. He tried unsuccessfully to snap the chute to his harness, but couldn't get either snap into place. Realizing he was about to strike the ground, he pulled with one hand and held on for dear life with the other. The chute was ripped from his hands but at that instant a snap caught in a D-ring and he found himself swinging lazily and safely under the inflated canopy, suspended by one ring.

A gunner and a radioman shared one parachute when they jumped together at 15,000 feet over Germany in 1943. The second man somehow managed to maintain his grip during the opening shock and hung on for more than ten minutes before his strength gave out and he fell the last few hundred feet to his death.

Probably the most incredible story (it's documented and true) is of Joe Herman and John Vivash. Herman was blown, without his parachute, from his exploding plane at 17,000 feet one dark night over Germany in 1944. Vivash was also blown out but had his parachute on. At about 5,000 feet, Vivash regained consciousness and opened his chute. Herman, fully conscious, bumped into Vivash's body and instinctively hung on. They floated down together on one parachute. They crashed through some brush, Herman on the bottom suffering a couple of broken ribs. They evaded capture for four days before the Germans caught them.

In some cases a jumper has been unable to get his parachute properly inflated and still has survived. Dr. Richard G. Snyder, for instance, has made a detailed study of a number of terminal velocity impacts into snow and other substances. It has been estimated that a partially inflated canopy will slow a jumper enough so he can survive in most cases. A canopy which fails to catch air (as when the sleeve fails to clear the canopy) and forms a streamer behind the jumper will still reduce the descent rate appreciably. Joseph Thrift jumped from 12,500 feet and came into a hayfield with a partially inflated canopy at an estimated 85 mph. He suffered a fractured back, cuts and bruises, and possible internal injuries—but survived. At the hospital, the doctors considered him to be in good condition.

One person who survived without a chute's assistance was Lt. Col. I. M. Chissov of the Soviet Air Force. Chissov had his plane shot out from under him during WW II by several German fighters. He bailed out. Fearing he would be riddled in the air if he opened at 23,000 feet, he decided to delay the opening down to 1,000 feet. During the fall, he lost consciousness and hit with his parachute still intact on a slope covered with some three feet of snow. When he regained consciousness fifteen minutes later, Russian soldiers had reached him, and he was taken to a hospital. He had suffered a fractured pelvis and concussion of the spine—and was out of the hospital in three and a half months. He is still active and made his 272nd parachute jump to celebrate his seventieth birthday!

Russian mechanic G. Ochepkov accidently opened the door of a helicopter and fell out at 1,060 feet. He had previously made twenty-seven parachute jumps but did not have a chute on when he fell through the door. Ochepkov assumed a horizontal face-to-earth position, then opened his heavy quilted jacket and held the flaps in an open position to trap air. Like a flying squirrel, he glided himself into a clearing in the woods which was covered with more than six feet of snow. He was knocked unconscious, but recovered consciousness when the helicopter landed and climbed, unaided, back into the craft.

During WW II both German and Russian troops were reported to have dropped from low-flying planes into deep snow without the aid of parachutes. Units of the German 4th Army reported to German Intelligence that they had witnessed Soviet troops spilling from low-flying troop carriers without the aid of parachutes during the Yukhnov airborne operation of 1942. One documented case reported that airborne troops were placed in sacks filled with straw!

In 1955, during a large airborne operation in Alaska, an observer saw what appeared to be an unsupported bundle falling from a C-119; no chute deployed from the object. The observer noted that the impact looked like a mortar round exploding in the snow. When aidmen arrived at the spot, they found a young Negro paratrooper flat on his back at the bottom of a three-foot hole in the snow. He could talk and appeared to be uninjured. However, they took him to a hospital where it was determined that he had two minor fractures and bruises. He rejoined his unit a few days later.

Again during WW II, Nicholas Alkemade, whose Lancaster bomber and parachute were aflame at 18,000 feet over Germany, decided he'd rather die falling than stay and burn to death in his plane. He turned his gun turret around, dropped out into the pre-dawn darkness on March 23, 1944, and plummeted 18,000 feet into a young pine tree. Crashing through the tree, he slammed into eighteen inches of snow that had drifted up under it. There was no snow on the ground except under the tree. He not only lived; he wasn't even seriously injured. Regaining consciousness about three hours after bailing out, he stood up, lit a cigarette, and thanked his lucky stars. After his capture he was treated for burns and had splinters and twigs removed from his flesh. Because he had no parachute, he was accused of being a spy who had hidden his chute. A check of his harness revealed that the liftwebs of the harness he wore (QAC harness) were still tacked down by break cord, indicating the parachute had never been used. Later the wreckage of his plane was found along with the burned parachute still in its metal container beside the gun turret.

What if an airman at 40,000 feet opened his chute immediately on exit, rather than dropping down to lower and more livable air? At such an altitude the temperatures are seventy degrees below zero and oxygen is so scarce that death comes in a matter of seconds. An unintentional jump by Lieutenant Colonel W. R. Lovelace of the Army Air Corps provided some of the answers. Lovelace was not a parachute jumper—he had never made a parachute jump in his life. He was a doctor, a surgeon, to be specific. In 1943, he stepped through the open bomb bay of a B-17 Flying Fortress, where a static line immediately opened his parachute. Lovelace was knocked unconscious by the opening shock, his glove torn from his left hand.

Oscillating violently in sub-zero temperatures, his hand froze during the long, tortuous descent. The oscillation continued during the entire descent and he suffered from extreme nausea as well as frostbite, shock, and oxygen starvation. While he proved that an airman could survive an opening and descent from that high altitude, his jump also proved the delayed drop to be preferable. The recommended procedure then, as it is today, was to ride the disabled plane down to safer air before bailing out or else delay opening until livable air is reached.

William Stannard, a gunner on a Ventura, was cut off from the exit by flames. Although he managed to get his chute, it was already burning and fell from its container in a melting glob. Flames forced him farther back into the rear of the plane. Finally wedged in the extreme tail section, he crouched in a ball with his legs drawn up to his chin and his hands over his face as the flames licked at him. Suddenly the last ten feet of fuselage and tail broke away and fell free of the flaming main section. Stannard found himself trapped inside the tail assembly that glided and fluttered like a leaf. He sat watching the skyline and countryside sweeping by during the 9,000 foot descent. The strange vehicle crashed through some pine trees and, as it ground to a halt, Stannard tumbled out—dazed but not seriously hurt.

Peter Underdown rode his ejection seat (the parachute never deployed) through an orchard grove in 1954. When his Sabre broke up in flight, his seat broke loose (it was not fired). He smashed through the orchard where his seat—with him still in it—wedged in the fork of an apple tree. He was conscious and yelling, but has no recollection of the three days following the flight. His plane broke up at an estimated 400 mph and he hurtled 2,000 feet to the ground. The trajectory of his seat coincided with the slope of the hill so that the seat struck tree after tree, slowing down until it finally wedged in the forks of the apple tree.

Test pilot, George Franklin Smith of Manhattan Beach, California, was the first man to make an emergency jump flying from an airplane at supersonic speed. He ejected from an F-100A Super Sabre jet fighter on February 26, 1955, at an altitude of 6,500 feet and a speed of 777 mph. He experienced a deceleration of forty G's as the windblast cut his clothes to ribbons and his shoes, socks, helmet, and oxygen mask were stripped away. His parachute was torn in several places but safely lowered the unconscious and half-dead Smith into the ocean off Los Angeles where he was rescued by a passing boat. He was hospitalized for six months, but survived to fly again. The need for some type of protection during a supersonic bail-out was obvious, and Smith's experience spurred the development of a supersonic ejection system.

In an effort to cope with emergency conditions at supersonic speeds, parachute manufacturers strengthened their parachutes and escape systems. However, with parachutes already able to withstand greater forces than the human body, making the chute even stronger was meaningless. To develop an emergency system that will work instantly when a pilot is ejecting a sluggish plane that falters or fails during takeoff and at very low speeds was difficult, but possible. A number of successful systems were developed. Jim Hall proved a system that would work at zero altitude and zero airspeed. To develop a system that would work at supersonic speeds was also difficult, but possible. Developing a system that would work rapidly at both low altitude and slow speeds, yet work slowly at high altitudes and high speeds . . . well. Unlike the sport jumper who chooses his speed and altitude, the luckless airman who hits the silk to save his life must go when conditions require it—no matter how fast or how slow and no matter how high or how low.

Until the supersonic era, the same parachute and same over-the-side technique would work under any situation, but based upon experiences of those few who made emergency exits at near supersonic speeds and lived to tell of it, new methods of escape and new escape systems had to be developed.

Airplane manufacturers began designing new escape systems that would allow more protection at high speeds; parachute manufacturers worked closely with the airplane industry to customize parachutes and automatic devices for opening the parachutes. After dummy tests indicated success, it was up to a handful of dedicated men to make live tests. These test jumpers set out to prove they had a solution to the emergency jumper's problems—and the test jumpers staked their lives that they were right.

3 WILL IT WORK? Test Jumping

Test jumping is more than just strapping on a chute and jumping with it. There was a time when this was the case—when Irvin jumped and proved a free-fall pack would work and when Lieutenant R. A. Caldwell jumped and proved his static arrangement *would not* (it fouled and he was killed).

If the chute opened and held together, the design was considered a success; if it didn't, they simply buried the victim and tried some other design. But that was fifty years ago. Chutes were so unreliable then that few were used during WW I.

Test groups and individuals worked steadily in the succeeding years to develop not only reliable chutes, but other lifesaving equipment and techniques of escape. Planes were going faster and higher—that meant bailouts might be made at great speeds and above the region of breathable air. Parachutes had to be strengthened to withstand high-speed openings or modified in such a way that the parachute would open more slowly. By the end of WW II, parachute components no longer needed to be strengthened—the parachute would hold together longer than the man using it.

During WW II, the Germans developed the jet airplane. Bail-out at jet speeds using a standard quick-opening parachute was, to say the least, uncomfortable . . . and to say the most, fatal. They developed the deployment sleeve that is now commonly used in sport parachuting. A sleeve allowed the airman time to get into a proper position as it slowed his body. The sleeve, encasing the canopy, slowed the opening of the canopy so the lines could deploy and the airman could be pulled into the proper position for inflation. The deployment bag operated on the same principle and found its way into paratroop rigs—the T-10—and various emergency parachutes.

As speeds increased it became impossible for an airman to open a hatch and jump out. Ejection seats came into use. High-altitude exits meant the airman needed to carry an oxygen supply, the bailout bottle, or learn the techniques of falling to lower altitudes and breathable air. Pressure suits were developed to keep the man alive above his physical limits. Higher and higher, faster and faster . . . each development brought new escape problems. Each escape problem brought new equipment. New equipment had to be tested and proved. New techniques of exit and of fall had to be developed. Somebody had to prove to pilots that bailing out was safer than crashing with the plane.

In the early 1920's, the odds for survival in an emergency jump were about 50–50; odds for surviving a crash with the plane were about the same. Major E. L. Hoffman and his test group at McCook Field had determined that a free-falling body reaches a terminal velocity (when the pull of gravity is equal to the wind resistance) of about 120 mph after falling roughly 1,500 feet. They reasoned, then, that if the pilot bailed out at high speed he would actually slow down as he fell. If he could delay his opening for a brief time, he would be slowing down until he reached 120 mph. In the higher, thinner air, he would fall faster but as he dropped into the denser air of lower altitudes he would continue to slow down until a tolerable opening speed was reached. The theory sounded good, but nobody had made a delayed free fall . . . yet.

Irvin had made a free-fall jump, but how far did he fall before he opened? Just far enough to clear the plane—no more.

Pilots and the public in general still had the notion that a delayed fall would result in death or unconsciousness. Besides, slide-rule calculations are one thing—actual performance is something else!

Sgt. Randall Bose decided to prove delayed free falls could be accomplished safely. He delayed his opening for 1,500 feet on one jump and later delayed for 1,800 feet—the first recorded delayed free falls. These jumps were not entirely in the official capacity of test jumper, but more in the form of a bet with some friends who didn't believe it could be done. He made believers of them, collecting on his bet. Bose learned something during his first delayed fall that nobody was aware of—wierd things begin to happen at terminal velocity.

His fall was controlled for the first ten seconds, but suddenly everything went crazy. He found himself gyrating, buffeting, swaying from side to side, and generally losing his equilibrium. He even flipped over a couple times. On his next jump, he was waiting for it, but could do nothing to stop it except pull his ripcord. Although Bose had fallen at terminal velocity only a few seconds, these seconds were enough to prove that "something" happens beyond that twelfth second. Had he fallen another ten seconds he would have encountered the flat spin.

Test jumpers today are aware of the spin and fight it off before it can occur, just as sport jumpers must do. The human body tends to rotate at terminal velocity like a runaway propeller. If the spin is allowed to continue, centrifugal force takes over and the arms and legs are pulled away from the body. In this spread-eagle position, blood is forced away from the center (the body's trunk) into the arms and legs and head. A red-out (unconsciousness) results.

Spins are erratic, though, and a shifting of the body can cause it to stop and even to counter-rotate. Understanding what makes the body spin is the first step in preventing or correcting one. One foot or leg higher or lower, one arm or hand higher or lower than the other, or the body twisted slightly—each can cause a spin; there are other factors, but these are basic. In advanced free-fall maneuvers, the jumper learns to use these movements to make turns to the left or right—in competition judging he must do them rapidly and precisely.

The automatic opener is a significant device used to reduce deaths from spins. Most parachutes in use by the military are now equipped with an opener that pulls the ripcord automatically at a given altitude. Depending on the elevation of terrain over which the airman is flying, these openers are normally set to barometrically activate at elevations from 5,000 to 17,000 feet. If the airman bails out below the altitude set on his opener, a timing mechanism pulls the ripcord on the chute. This timer is usually activated automatically as the airman separates from the seat. Timers can be set from as low as five seconds to as much as fifteen seconds. (They can be modified for sport use for greater delay.) The time is necessary to allow the airman to slow down from his initial speed at bailout. If a pilot ejects at high altitude, he simply relys on his automatic opener to take over at the proper time. If he gets in an uncontrollable spin and loses consciousness or cannot pull his ripcord, the automatic opener will do it for him. Although an opening during a flat spin results in twisted suspension lines and often friction burns on the canopy, the lines normally unwind quickly and the canopy inflates properly. Test jumpers learned early in the game that if they encountered a spin that could not be controlled or kept within tolerable limits, the ripcord should be pulled. This is a good rule for sport jumpers to remember, too.

After Bose made those first delayed free falls and had a brief brush with the effects of terminal velocity, other test jumpers pushed on for answers to other questions. Other men experimented with delayed fall—men like Art Starnes and Russia's Boris Kharakhonoff. Starnes made a free fall from 30,800 feet loaded with nearly 100 pounds of equipment that included, in addition to his two parachutes, a stopwatch, an altimeter, a shortwave radio, a 16 mm movie camera, various medical sensors, and other odds and ends. The six-mile free-fall record that he set in 1940 was broken the next year by Kharakhonoff's drop from 40,813 feet. Both men proved that free falls from high altitudes could be made safely.

Although testing parachute equipment is done by various manufacturers, a great deal of testing is done by the military since they are the major user. Certain specifications are laid down by the federal government and the manufacturers must adhere to these specifications. When the manufacturer—whether he be the maker of an entire assembly or only a part of it—turns it over to the various military organizations, the equipment receives additional testing. Usually this testing is done in a cooperative effort between the manufacturer and the military all during the development. For project engineers representing half a dozen rival manufacturers to work cooperatively at the same installation is not unusual. While the manufacturer is anxious to win the contract, he is also vitally concerned that his equipment be safe, operational, and proved, before being put into everyday use.

For more than thirty years, the major parachute testing operations were conducted at McCook Field, Dayton, Ohio, where Irvin made the world's first free-fall jump to prove the Model A parachute would work. The results of his test made parachutes acceptable to the military and optional for all pilots. When young Lieutenant Harold Harris bailed out and saved his life with that same type parachute in 1922, he proved that the parachute would not only work, but that it was practical for pilots in an emergency. The results of Lieutenant Harris' experience made parachutes mandatory a year later.

In 1952, the parachute test center was moved to El Centro, California, where it is today. This was done to consolidate the efforts of the Air Force with those of the Navy at the Navy Auxiliary Air Station in El Centro. The unit became the Joint Department of Defense Parachute Testing Center, (although each service has its own test projects, they share facilities and, frequently, personnel).

Four men's names are synonymous with parachute testing there. They worked together for fifteen years and have become known as "the jumping warrants" as each climbed the promotion ladder to become chief warrant officers.

Lawrence Lambert started parachuting as a flying circus barnstormer before entering the service. He received the Cheney Award for his outstanding work testing the first USAF ejection seat system. He later worked with Colonel John P. Stapp in the deceleration tests at old Muroc Air Base and, still later, assisted in training Captain Joe Kittinger who went on to set the world's unofficial record high-altitude jump.

Victor A. James, who also made his first jump at an air show, went on to test the overall ejection system with a high-speed bailout from a P-80 jet. He also set a high-altitude record free fall (for the 1950's) by bailing out at 38,000 feet and free falling 24,000 feet before opening his chute. The tests were made to determine if a man should free fall with or without his seat to his opening altitude.

Mitchell Kanowski began jumping at Airborne Infantry School at Ft. Benning, Georgia, where one of his duties was testing captured enemy parachutes. At El Centro he went on to test the German ribbon design which was ultimately adopted and used in the experimental high-altitude research rocket planes.

Isadore Rosenberg was the only one to begin his testing career as just that—a test jumper. He volunteered at Wright-Patterson Air Force Base after seeing a notice on the bulletin board asking for volunteers to take part in some parachute testing programs. His contributions, in addition to test jumping himself, include numerous designs and modifications for survival in low-altitude escapes from both jet and conventional propeller-driven craft.

There are dozens of others who are highly respected and experienced. Self-sacrifice has been a characteristic of test jumpers since the beginning. The development of safe equipment to save the lives of others remains their first concern and their own skins take second place. When the exhibition jumper attempts some hare-brained stunt, he gets money and glory. When a test jumper does something even more spectacular, he gets little more than experience and a sense of satisfaction.

Before live-test jumps are made on a new design, it is tested on machines and on dummy drops. Although instrumented dummies are used in the initial phases of development of any parachute or escape system, ultimately a human being must prove equipment. There are two main reasons for this. First, an instrumented dummy does not fall or respond like a human being and no amount of instrumentation can detect every minute detail of performance. Second, no pilot or airman wearing this equipment likes to think it works only in theory on the drawing board or on a dummy. He wants to know it has been proved by many successful jumps by real, live people.

The Vortex Ring Parachute was designed by David Barish who also designed the Barish Sailwing. The Vortex Ring chute looks more like a ragged malfunction than a parachute and has all the characteristics of a rotating Mae West. Designed for non-personal use, twelve live tests were made to see what potential existed for sport use. Jaques Istel made two jumps with it at the Orange Sport Parachute Center and had to cut away from one malfunction. Nate Pond made ten jumps into Long Island Sound off New London, Connecticut. Pond chose to jump over water after seeing how hard Istel landed on earlier jumps. There were two risers from the harness going up to a ball-bearing swivel about three feet above his head. The parachute rotates as it descends, and the jumper tends to counter-rotate unless he can extend his arms and deflect air with the hands to control the spinning, as Pond discovered. Pond had to cut away from one malfunction out of ten jumps and reported that if one of the wings malfunctioned, it would tangle with the others due to the rotation.

Vince Mazza made the first jet ejection from a P-80 and later made a record-breaking parachute drop from 42,176 feet. On that jump he weighed 347 pounds, including his equipment. Ed Sperry and Hank Neilsen broke Mazza's record when they made some downward ejections in 1954 from an altitude of 45,200 feet. Others working on the downward ejection seat then were Chic Henderson and George Post.

Sergeant George Post received the Distinguished Flying Cross for his part in these first downward ejections. He was the first enlisted man to leave a B-47 jet bomber by that method. He and fellow test jumpers, Captain Harry Collins and Ray Madson, made numerous high-altitude bailouts and went on to test equipment used on extremely high altitudes.

While working with Raven Industries in the manufacture of the strato-jump balloon, Nick Piantanida also test jumped some unique plastic parachutes developed by Raven. These parachutes designated "Raven-Plus" are inexpensive, very stable, extremely lightweight, and range in size from eight inches in diameter to eighty feet. Raven has also made parachutes of similar design in special plastic films that are water soluble. These are intended for applications to limited warfare and one-shot use. After a cargo drop, the canopies slowly degrade as atmospheric moisture is absorbed. Pictured here is Nick descending in the 37½-foot R-Plus parachute during testing and evaluation.

Another experiment at Raven Industries, developed by senior engineer Russell A. Pohl, offers the pilot a choice of parachute or balloon. It was designed to help rescue pilots shot down over North Vietnam or other enemy territory. The pilot will eject and after his seat falls away, pull a ripcord to inflate a hot-air balloon. The balloon will carry him up to 5,000 feet where he will wait for a recovery plane to pick him up. The recovery system, conducted by C-130 cargo planes, has been successfully accomplished by using two 35-foot steel poles and a hook and loop assembly. The rescue pilot flys the recovery plane over the downed airman, and the balloon collapses as the hook and loop assembly engage it. An energy-absorbing winch in the recovery plane takes the shock and then reels the pilot and collapsed balloon aboard. Plans called for the ballon to be inflated with air by the fall of the airman, then a bottle of compressed propane gas would begin burning automatically. The hot air would fill the bag, slow the descent to a stop, and then lift the airman to the 5,000-foot level.

In another experiment, Charles M. Alexander volunteered to test a technique of midair recovery of a parachute. In September, 1966, Alexander, a project engineer for Pioneer, became the first person to be recovered from midair. He jumped at 9,000 feet and was recovered at 8,000 feet by pilot Arnold Olsen, flying a C-122 for All American Engineering Company, manufacturer of the airborne retrieval equipment.

Extending up from Alexander's modified C-9 main canopy was a nylon load line seventy-feet long with a breaking strength of 4,000 pounds. At the upper end of the line was an eleven-foot diameter guide surface target or engagement chute that was snagged by the recovery plane. The special energy-absorbing line and winch were the secret of the system's success.

Other systems are being tested by which a downed pilot could be recovered from midair by any of his fellow fighter pilots flying the same mission over enemy territory. Engaging hooks could be installed on all aircraft but without the winch or recovery system. The parachutist would simply be towed back to friendly territory and then released. His parachute would rein-flate (successful tests have already been made) and he would descend to safety. In another similar experiment by All American Engineering, the downed pilot can be recovered from the ground by tossing the recovery line over a couple of small trees where the recovery plane can swoop low and engage the line. This system became operational in Vietnam.

All American developed a specially treated nylon they call "Unolyn" for their recovery line. It can stretch 200– to 300 percent to absorb shock and then remain elongated. Other elastic lines of rubber or nylon spring back with catapulting effects. Since this recovery line is permanently elongated, it can be used only once. However, the Unolyn material is inexpensive and after one use, can be discarded and replaced with a new section of line.

There are obviously too many test jumpers—military and civilian—to begin to discuss them all. Certain ones stand out for special achievements that should be recognized here. I have had the good fortune and pleasure of personally meeting and jumping with some of the nation's top test jumpers; there is no finer group of men alive today.

One such man is Sergeant James A. Howell, USAF. He is one of many dedicated men who has served in the USAF 6511th Test Group (P) NAF, El Centro, California. The 6511th is part of the Air Force flight test center, AF systems command, Edwards AFB, California.

On June 6, 1961, Howell became the first man to live-test the supersonic ejection seat. He ejected from an F-106B inter-ceptor travelling at 558 mph at 22,000 feet over Holloman AFMDC, New Mexico. The ejection seat used in this test was the F-106 advanced escape system commonly known as the "B" seat, or supersonic seat. The test was an unqualified success that climaxed a four-and-a-half-year program to develop a safe pilot escape system for high-speed aircraft. Less than five months later, he made the first live-test ejection of the toboggan-like rescue vehicle. One of the best liked and most respected men in the business of test jumping, Howell had twice been awarded the Distinguished Flying Cross.

Early in 1956 the need for a high-speed escape system was

reaching a critical stage as faster and faster planes were being developed. The Air Force requested the aircraft industry to join with equipment manufacturers to develop such a system. The group was known as the Industry Crew Escape Systems Committee and consisted of representatives from fourteen aircraft and equipment companies. The seat that resulted from their labors had the unique feature of rotating backward as it emerged from the aircraft so that when launched, the pilot was in a supine position. It was propelled away from the aircraft by a rocket and stabilized against tumbling by two long three-inch diameter booms extending aft along the flight path. The action of these booms was similar to that of the stick on a skyrocket.

After the ejection, Howell plummeted 7,000 feet in a 40-second free fall until an explosive charge—triggered by barometric pressure—cut the shoulder straps and lap belts holding him to the seat. It also fired a weight that pulled out a small parachute. The small chute hoisted Howell from the seat and opened a conventional parachute on his back. Eight minutes after beginning his 4½-mile drop—his four hundredth for the Air Force—he was on the ground.

Sergeant Thomas H. Rolf is one of the men who shared the earlier testing with Howell. He rode the seat down a tilting steel and wood rack and out the back of a C-130 Lockheed Hercules cargo plane. These were test drops prior to installation systems for actual ejections. Some of the work done by test jumpers is classified and cannot be released to the general public.

Testing a variety of the multistage personnel parachutes that are used by our astronauts was a job that fell to other test jumpers such as Sergeant William E. Powers, Jr. and Sergeant Richard Marcum, the two top jumpers in the country, according to fellow jumper Howell. Pictured here is Sergeant Powers in the Gemini pressure suit and gear just prior to a drop.

These test drops were unusually complex, involving extremes in altitude, with multistage, four-timer-systems, all self-contained and both fully automatic or manually operated. On this particular drop, shortly after his exit, he experienced a malfunction in his first stage chute, then his main also failed. The plastic

Sgt. Wlliam E. Powers, Jr., in the Gemini pressure suit and gear just prior to a drop. On this drop his parachutes malfunctioned and the plastic mouth cover made breathing nearly impossible. He somehow overcame the problems and landed safely. (*U.S. Air Force*)

No matter how good it looks on a drawing board, every new design ultimately must be live-tested by a test jumper. A test jumper must possess an abundance of courage as well as skill and experience if he is to thoroughly evaluate the flight characteristics and offer constructive suggestions for improvement. Here Lee Guilfoyle flys an early Barish Sailwing design. (*Jerry Irwin*)

Sgt. James A. Howell is shown shortly after his test drop of the B-seat ejection system in September, 1960. A few months later, he became the first person to live-test the ejection system at a speed of 558 mph. Howell has twice been awarded the Distinguished Flying Cross for his outstanding work. (*U.S. Air Force*)

Before the test jumper puts a new design to the acid test and makes a live jump on it, machines such as this whirl tower are used to check strength, stability, and other vital characteristics. Wind tunnel tests are also made. (*Pioneer Parachute Co.*)

Late astronaut Virgil Grissom is pictured with the Pioneer Parasail. Towed behind a boat, the Parasail lifts like a kite, but descends like a standard parachute. (*NASA*)

Jim Hall tests the F-106 ejection seat in a zero-zero situation. He wore no reserve parachute since there would be no time to use it if the system failed. Hall is a recipient of the Leo Stevens award for his contributions to safe parachuting. (*Parachuting Associates, Inc.*)

Ralph Weekly rides an ejection seat out the tailgate of a USAF C-130 to test the separation sequence. Exiting on either side are free-fall photographers Bud Kiesow (left) and Bob Sinclair (right) who documented the action with motion picture film. (*Parachuting Associates, Inc.*)

Charles Alexander with the parachutes worn for the world's first midair recovery of a human being. The small pack on his chest above the reserve chute contains an 11-foot target parachute attached to a 70-foot shock-absorbing line. The other end of the line is attached to the apex of his main canopy. The recovery plane snagged the target chute and then reeled Alexander in like a fish. Chuck is a master parachute rigger, commercial pilot, and University of Colorado graduate. He received the Leo Stevens medal for 1966, parachuting's highest award, for this work. (*All American Engineering*)

Pioneer Parachute Company engineer Charles Alexander, with more than 860 jumps, is reeled into the plane after the world's first human midair recovery. (*All American Engineering*)

Nate Pond is seen here making one of several test jumps on the Vortex Ring parachute designed by David Barish. Pond made this jump into Long Island Sound off New London, Connecticut. (*Pioneer Parachute Co.*)

Nick Piantanida made the first manned jump of a plastic film parachute and reported it to be very stable. By pulling down on a riser of this 37.5-foot model, he demonstrated a controlled 360-degree turn in ten seconds. (*Raven Industries, Inc.*)

Loy Brydon, the first American to log 1,000 free falls, makes the first live-test jump of the Rogallo Parawing, an all-flexible deployable glider. From this basic design a number of modifications have been developed. (*Irvin Para-Space Center*)

The solid Parawing was one of the first of the high-performance designs, but openings were severe. Irvin Para-Space Center and Steve Snyder Enterprises worked together to develop a satisfactory deployment system. (*Irvin Para-Space Center*)

The slotted Parawing was an improvement over the earlier solid models, giving stability and lift to the wing. (*Irvin Para-Space Center*)

The Ballute is test-jumped by Col. Clyde S. Cherry, commanding officer of the 6511th Test Group (Parachute) at the Naval Air Facility, El Centro, California. Recording the action with his helmet-mounted camera is Chief Warrant Officer Charles O. Laine. (*Goodyear*)

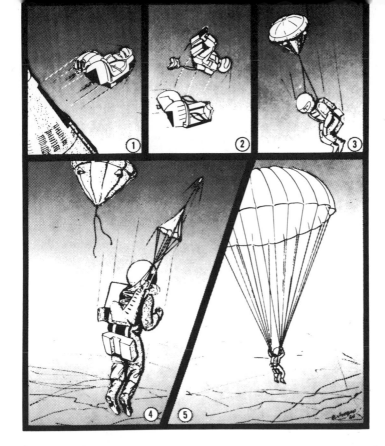

This schematic drawing shows the sequence of events if our **Gemini** astronauts had been forced to eject during launch or reentry. Apollo pilots wore no parachutes and relied on the escape rocket to pull them free to an altitude where the three main canopies could safely lower the entire spacecraft. (*Goodyear*)

mouth cover taped over his nose began sticking to his face making breathing almost impossible. He was tumbling out of control. Because of his full-pressure spacesuit and survival kits, his movements were hampered. He could not free his breathing because of the space helmet and faceplate and his malfunctioned equipment wrapped him into a neat package. He somehow managed to keep a cool head and quickly corrected his difficulties.

Sergeant Powers does not limit his parachuting to only testing —which he began back in 1958. He has been active in the sport of parachuting, a member of the Parachute Club of America (now USPA), an area safety officer, holder of a D-license (expert), and organizer-instructor of local clubs.

There is little comparison between sport jumping equipment and techniques and those involved in testing. The sport jumper usually drops from a slow plane, often at less than 10,000 feet, and opens at 2,500 feet to 1,800 feet with a sleeve- or bag-deployed chute that requires three to four seconds to completely inflate. The test jumper may drop from extremely high altitudes and at high speeds and have his chute opened instantly by a ballistic slug at no less than 14,500 feet! It is generally agreed that opening shock is greater at higher altitudes than in lower, denser air. Howell and others of his group made these drops in standard 28-foot flat circular canopies without any deployment bag or sleeve. Where there is little discomfort during the opening of a sport parachute, the test jumper sometimes wears a protective metal-frame chest protector to keep his ribs from being crushed during the opening of some chutes, particularly when wearing the reserve parachute. The windblast alone is sometimes great enough during high-speed ejections to require extra protection of the jumper. Reserves must be shielded by a windblast cover that is automatically released after the jumper's speed has decelerated. Some test jumpers have tested equipment without the benefit of the reserve because it would not have time to deploy if the main malfunctioned.

Such a man is James C. Hall, for many years an executive of ParaVentures and later Parachuting Associates, Inc., of Los Angeles. He has been a professional parachutist for more than twenty years. Hall made the first human test of the free world's only operational zero altitude-zero airspeed ejection seat, developed by the Weber Aircraft Company. In one year, 1964, thirty-five airmen were killed during takeoff or landing when their aircraft developed trouble on the runway. In many cases the pilots ejected but their escape systems could not operate in time.

Hall set out to prove that this zero-zero system would work in time. He initiated the entire sequence by pulling the ejection handle of his seat in a simulated cockpit as it sat stationary, anchored to the ground. An explosive charge shot him straight up from the cockpit. As he cleared the cockpit, a 4,500-pound thrust rocket burned for less than a second to shove him 400 feet into the air in forward flight at an angle of about sixty degrees. Within two seconds after leaving the ground-based platform, the seat and man automatically separated. The parachute deployment gun fired a thirteen-ounce slug that extracted a small drogue chute and the main 28-foot diameter chute inflated. He was hanging about 350 feet in the air; some 400 feet horizontally from his blast-off point. Twenty-five seconds after ejection, he landed safely in a small pond. He had purposely chosen to be shot into the pond in the event anything failed, since he wore no reserve parachute and would not have had time to use it if he had.

A major in the Air Force Reserve, Hall is also recipient of the highest award in the field of parachuting safety—the Leo Stevens Parachute Medal. He received this for the development of an advanced free-fall parachuting instruction method and for perfecting the method.

Hall is co-inventor of the Air Force's emergency parachuting safety aid, the "four line cut" parachute canopy modification. By cutting the two inside suspension lines on each rear riser (numbers two and one; twenty-eight and twenty-seven) a standard 28-foot canopy developes steerable characteristics so the airman can avoid dangerous obstacles and steer his canopy by pulling down on left or right risers.

In addition to his testing of equipment and techniques, Hall has been active in all phases of professional parachuting, teaming with another highly respected parachutist, Dave Burt, in forming ParaVentures several years ago.

One of the recent developments in parachuting is the Parawing, invented by Dr. Francis Rogallo, aerodynamicist for NASA. Loy Brydon, D-12 (the twelfth recipient of the Class D-expert license), the first American to make 1,000 free falls and developer of free-fall techniques and parachute modifications, made the first live-test jump of the Rogallo Parawing—an all-flexible deployable glider-like parachute. He made the first test in March, 1966 at Fort Bragg, N.C. Others participating in the evaluation jumps were Lieutenant Jack Helms, Captain James Perry, M/Sgt. Harry Lewis, and S/Sgt. Richard Peyton.

Pioneer Parachute Company built two wings for testing, while Irvin Para-Space Center built two others of slightly different design. Sergeant Lewis made the first live test of the Irvin design. The Irvin Parawing may be the best competition chute yet. Irvin engineer Ed Drumheller gives much credit to fellow jumper-engineer Steve Snyder, of Steve Snyder Enterprises, for developing an acceptable deployment device. The earlier models gave severe opening shock.

Early in 1964, tests were made to evaluate the Ballute as a safety device for the Gemini astronauts. Goodyear Aerospace developed the Ballute device under contract to McDonnell Aircraft Corporation, prime contractor for NASA's Project Gemini. The aluminum-coated, nylon device inflates to 48 inches in diameter and acts as a stabilizer until the astronaut reaches an altitude where the conventional parachute is deployed. During training for the Gemini mission, astronauts were required to make several parachute descents into water to test survival techniques. Although NASA did not require any actual parachute jumps, they did require extensive training in parachute descents. The Parasail—billed as "the parachute that goes up" —which lifts like a kite when towed behind a boat, but descends like a standard parachute, was used.

The accompanying drawing shows the sequence of events if the Gemini astronauts had been forced to eject during launch or reentry traveling at up to three times the speed of sound. (1) Astronaut is ejected from spacecraft and (2) separated from seat as Goodyear's Ballute is deployed; (3) Ballute stabilizes him in feet-down position and slows his descent; (4) Ballute is jettisoned at approximately 7,500 feet, and (5) conventional parachute is deployed. This system was never used, of course, and later Apollo aircraft relied on the escape tower and the spacecraft's parachutes in the event of trouble. Astronauts on Apollo missions wore no parachutes.

Cool action under the most extreme stress situations exemplifies the skill and courage of the test jumper. He meets every challenge, every danger, with a sense of determination to prove or disprove the worth of a particular design. Daredevils of the circuses—with their human cannonball acts or highwire stunts —are putting on a show before thousands of people who will pay large sums of money and applaud thunderously. The test jumper puts on his "act" before a handful of people in the air and on the ground—and his pay is small.

4 HOW HIGH THE SKY
High-Altitude Jumping

Who made the first high-altitude jump is a difficult question to answer, since the term is relative. What was a high-altitude jump only thirty years ago is commonplace now among hundreds of sport parachutists.

Among the highest emergency bailouts were those made by John de Salis and Patrick Lowe. Flying in a Canberra jet bomber over Derbyshire, England, in April, 1958, their plane exploded at 56,000 feet. Both men free fell down to 10,000 feet where their parachutes were automatically opened.

Lieutenant Colonel W. R. Lovelace's static-line jump made at 40,000 feet (see Chapter II) deserves special recognition, not only from the fact that the long and tortuous descent nearly killed him, but that he had never made a parachute jump before in his life. The higher and faster planes of WW II made some type of escape from high altitude mandatory. Brave men risked their lives to find the answers.

On November 16, 1959, Captain Joseph William Kittinger, Jr., 32, set a high-altitude record parachute jump when he free fell from a balloon-supported open gondola 76,400 feet over the Air Force Missile Development Center, Holloman Air Force Base, New Mexico. It was not his first—he had made one emergency bailout and nearly fifty intentional jumps—but it was very nearly his last. This was the first of three extremely high jumps in Project Excelsior intended to test high-altitude bailout survival clothing and equipment in a special biospace research task developed by the Air Research and Development Command.

On the Excelsior I jump, Kittinger stepped out at 76,000 feet—5,000 feet higher than a man had even been in an open gondola. At 60,000 feet his body reached a terminal velocity of 423 mph. The outside air was 104 degrees below zero. Something happened to his stabilization chute and it tangled around his body where it fluttered uselessly. Kittinger controlled his body as much as he could in the thin air, but this was not enough and, despite all his efforts, he found himself building up into a deadly flat spin. He found himself paralyzed by the centrifugal force whirling him around and eventually he lost consciousness. When he regained consciousness, he was floating safely to earth under his automatically deployed reserve parachute. His automatically-opened main had fouled in the stabilization chute, then his reserve automatically deployed and tangled with the main. The reserve chute's pilot chute caught, preventing the canopy from inflating. However, Francis Beaupre, designer of the stabilization chute and Leo Stevens Medal winner, had anticipated such an emergency and substituted a weaker bridle cord from the apex to the pilot chute. This bridle cord broke when forces of falling built up, and the reserve canopy pulled free where it inflated properly.

Later examination showed that Kittinger had accidentally started his timer on his stabilization chute without realizing it when he stood up to jump. He delayed exit some ten or eleven seconds starting cameras and pulling other releases. When he stepped from the gondola, instead of having sixteen seconds of fall before the pilot chute would pop and deploy his six-foot stabilization chute, he had only two or three. This was not sufficient time to build up the speed needed to properly extend and inflate the chute. It simply bobbled around his body and entangled itself completely before speed built up to a functional level and, by then, it was too late.

Kittinger went up to make Excelsior II flight and jump just twenty-five days after the first. This time everything went exactly as planned. Exactly fourteen seconds after stepping out, he had reached a speed of 300 mph. His timer went off, the stabilization chute deployed perfectly. He fell in a perfectly stable position down to 18,000 feet where his main canopy deployed and lowered him to the ground 12 minutes and 32 seconds after exit. With Excelsior II going perfectly, he moved on the Excelsior III—the big one.

On August 16, 1960, Kittinger reached an altitude of 102,800 feet. Excelsior III had taken him higher than any man had ever been in a balloon. Taking part in Project Manhigh in 1957, he made the first ascent in a sealed gondola and reached 96,000 feet, followed later by Lieutenant Colonel David G. Simons who reached 102,000 feet. Lieutenant Clifton McClure, in the same project, later reached 99,000 feet, but these three flights were in enclosed gondolas. This time the pilot was completely exposed to the elements except for his pressurized spacesuit and survival equipment.

The equipment Kittinger wore on this jump exactly duplicated his weight—150 pounds. His 300-pound bulk required the efforts of several assistants as well as himself when he entered the open gondola. However, at 102,800 feet he weighed three pounds less. Gravity decreases one percent for each 100,-000 feet of altitude.

Like an overstuffed teddy bear, Kittinger struggled to his feet, shuffled to the doorway and hopped out nearly twenty miles above New Mexico.

Sixteen seconds after leaving the gondola of Excelsior III, a timer fired to release the Beaupre stabilization parachute. The six-foot diameter parachute had no visible effect on his fall—no shock—and he wondered if it was working or if he should pull his manual override. Then he felt the gentle tugging that assured him the chute was out and working properly—he was no longer doing a slow roll but had stabilized in a face-to-earth position. Thirty seconds after his exit he passed through the 90,000-foot mark and reached his top speed of 614 mph! He spoke into his tape recorder as he fell, giving readings from the stopwatch and altimeter and making remarks on the overall situation, his feelings, and the functioning of the automatic equipment. His chute, a standard 28-foot back pack, automatically deployed at 18,000 feet after he had fallen for four and one half minutes. As he reached the 1,000-foot level, he released some of his 150 pounds of equipment where a static-line deployed parachute lowered it separately to the desert floor. Kittinger landed in the soft warm sand 13 minutes and 45 seconds after exit. His jump had gone so perfectly that the follow-up jump by Sergeant Post was cancelled as unnecessary. He had proved that man and equipment can function and survive from the hostile realm of outer space.

An ironic note is the fact that, although both his balloon ascent and his jump were record-breakers, they could not be officially recognized as such. To set an official balloon record, the occupant must both ascend and descend in the balloon; Joe had not. To set an official parachute record, designated representatives of FAI must witness the jump and special recording barographs must be carried on the drop and neither of these requirements had been met. Kittinger's goal was not to set official records or gain personal glory; it was to test equipment. He accomplished that.

Ordinarily, a jump such as Kittinger's could only be made by military people, working for Uncle Sam and supported by millions of federal dollars, but Nicholas J. Piantanida, 33, was no ordinary man. He became interested in the problems of high-altitude bailouts and decided to do some testing on his own. He wanted to prove that a jumper, employing ordinary skydiving techniques of controlled free fall, could safely make the jump without any stabilization chute. He intended to break the speed of sound with nothing but his six-foot-two-inch, two-hundred-pound body. This sounded pretty hazardous to most people, but Nick began recruiting support for his project.

While it was true that Nick was not a trained astronaut or military test jumper, he was not entirely inexperienced or unfamiliar with the subject of flight and parachuting. He was a licensed pilot, rated for single-engine, multi-engine, and balloons. He had more than 400 parachute jumps to his credit and held a Class D (expert) parachutist's license, but his greatest qualification was his determination. It began to pay off when he teamed up with parachuting's super salesman, Jacques Istel.

By August, 1965, SPACE Inc., was formed. It stood for Survival Programs Above Common Environment and consisted of three principals: Parachutes Incorporated, Pioneer Parachute Company, and Piantanida.

SPACE began working on the strato-jump project. For civilians to work up a program of this magnitude was unthinkable. The money required for training, parachutes, spacesuits, instruments, balloon, helium, and dozens of other items would be well beyond the reach of any private enterprise. Space representatives—Piantanida and Istel taking a major role—began listing their objectives, then sought out those companies who could best profit from the project. Strato-jump objectives were: (1) To establish that a trained parachutist can free fall from altitudes in excess of 100,000 feet without the use of stabilizing devices. (2) To investigate the effects of transonic speeds on the human body in free fall. (3) To gain for the United States the world's free-fall altitude parachuting record. (4) To surpass the manned-balloon altitude record.

SPACE went on to explain the value of these objectives. If they could prove that a properly trained man can free fall safely from great altitudes without any stabilization device, the current system of emergency procedures could be greatly simplified. Normally, in the event of an emergency, the airman rides his disabled aircraft (or part of it) down to altitudes of less than 30,000 feet before getting out. In the event of fire or structural failure this is not always possible. Special free-fall training could mean the difference of life and death and, aside from saving a man's life, our government cannot afford to lose its financial investment. They pointed to the fact that the U.S. had invested $6,500,000 in each astronaut.

What happens to a man when he breaks through the sound barrier with his body? The Pioneer Parachute Company engineers computed that on a jump from 120,000 feet, the parachutist should reach a maximum speed of approximately mach 1.1 (750 mph) in the vicinity of 90,000 feet. They pointed out that at speeds near and above mach 1, the air flow may

Capt. Joseph W. Kittinger gets a final check of equipment in the pre-dawn hours before his record-breaking balloon ascent and parachute jump. (*U.S. Air Force*)

Nearly 20 miles above New Mexico, Capt. Kittinger shields his eyes from the blinding sun just before his "long, lonely, leap." A thin sheet of gold carries an electric current through his face shield to prevent frosting and ice formation as well as protect him from the unfiltered rays of the sun. (*U.S. Air Force*)

Although Capt. Kittinger deployed a six-foot stabilization parachute after sixteen seconds of free fall, he continued to accelerate for the first thirty seconds and reached a top speed of 614 mph. It took him a total of 13 minutes and 45 seconds to cover the 102,800 feet. (*U.S. Air Force*)

Maj. John Garrity has his recording barograph removed by USPA official Billy Berry. Maj. Garrity and thirteen other Army and Air Force jumpers set a world's record when they dropped from 43,500 feet and were awarded the Distinguished Flying Cross. As team leader, Maj. Garrity wore white stripes on the back of his coveralls for identification by other team members who would locate him and join up in formation during the drop. (*U.S. Air Force*)

Three times Nick Piantanida attempted to reach the outer limits of our atmosphere where he planned to break the sonic barrier in free fall with no stabilization chute. He once reached 123,000 feet, but equipment failure foiled him and so his third attempt was fatal. (*SPACE, Inc.*)

differ from what is normally experienced in free fall. A safety device would be available, however. In the event control could not be maintained, a small drogue chute would be deployed to slow the free-fall speed and reduce the dynamic pressure against the jumper's body. General Electric's Re-Entry Systems Department in Philadelphia sent equipment and a team of engineers and technicians to measure the free-fall velocity precisely. This would be accomplished by a small transmitter mounted on the rear of the reserve parachute container and a receiver positioned on the ground.

In addition to the actual scientific and technical value of the jump, there was the nationalism felt by many concerned. The Russians still held the official high-altitude parachute record. Eugene Andreev set the record on November 1, 1962, near Volsk, Russia, when he jumped from 83,523.41 feet. Kittinger's jump was higher, but, because it was not properly monitored by the Federation Aeronautique Internationale, it was not accepted as an official record. Nor could SPACE, Inc., break the world's balloon record set in May, 1961, by Commander Malcolm D. Ross, USNR, when he reached an altitude of 113,739.9 feet. Although Nick would go higher, he must return with the balloon in order to establish an official balloon record. Nick would return by parachute instead. The idea picked up momentum and Piantanida's enthusiasm spread to others.

Nick took extensive training in preparation for his adventure. The Air Force cooperated to the extent that they furnished pressure-suit training and initial physiological training at Tyndall Air Force Base at Panama City, Florida. Considerable additional physiological training and a cold chamber run, at minus seventy-three degrees Fahrenheit, were received at the Civil Aeromedical Research Institute, Federal Aviation Administration, in Oklahoma City. His parachute training was conducted at Parachutes Incorporated's Lakewood Sport Parachuting Center at Lakewood, New Jersey. There, with the guidance of Lee Guilfoyle, the center's manager, and other staff people, Nick made high-altitude drops with and without his pressure suit and purposely practiced recovering from spins.

Meanwhile, Istel and other members of SPACE, Inc., were lining up the necessary equipment. Some items were donated outright, some were provided at cost or less. Piantanida's instrumentation included an electric control panel, an absolute pressure gauge for determining altitude, two temperature gauges to read both inside and outside air temperature, and a clock. The parachutes, harness, and containers were especially designed, manufactured, and furnished for the project by Pioneer Parachute Company of Manchester, Connecticut, a partner in SPACE, Inc. His main canopy was, of course, Pioneer's highly maneuverable, slow-descending, Para-Commander. The reserve was a 28-foot military type, modified for steering, if that became necessary. He also had a six-foot hemisflo drogue chute mounted in a tandem pack along with the main chute on his back—just in case it became necessary to use it. He wore the reserve on the front with an altimeter and stopwatch mounted on it.

The full pressure suit was basically an Air Force type, especially constructed and modified for this project by the David Clark Co., of Worcester, Massachusetts. David Clark also built NASA's Gemini suits. Nick wore electrically heated mittens and socks as well as a helmet with an electrically heated visor.

The Firewel Company of Buffalo, New York, furnished the oxygen systems. Four separate oxygen systems were designed and assembled for the project. Both main and reserve breathing systems were installed on board the gondola along with an oxygen ventilation system for cooling the suit in the event of a heat buildup. A bailout unit of oxygen was carried inside the main parachute container and was to be activated a few minutes prior to the actual jump.

Automatic openers were installed in both the main and reserve parachutes. Both were model FF-1, manufactured and provided for the project by U.S. Gauge, Sellersville, Pennsylvania. The main was set to activate at 6,500 feet, with the reserve set for 4,000 feet. If necessary, the openers could be overridden for a manual pull higher if the jumper found himself over a congested area and needed more time and maneuvering room in the sky.

Communications systems involved three radios—one main and two backup units. A command receiver was used to control the balloon functions and, via this receiver, ballast could be dropped or the flight terminated. Both Nick and the ground control people could operate these functions. During free fall, Nick was to transmit his reactions into a tape recorder carried in a pocket on the leg of his pressure suit.

Nick would make three attempts at his goal. All three would be unsuccessful. The last one, fatal.

Strato-Jump I was a flight launched from New Brighton, Minnesota, on October 22, 1965. The attempt ended when the 3,700,000-cubic-foot balloon burst over St. Paul, Minnesota. He had just passed the 22,700-foot level when a six-knot wind sheer caught his balloon and shredded it. A ground signal released the gondola from the burst balloon and it descended under the large parachute with Nick in it. At 10,000 feet, Nick decided to bail out and try to steer his personnel chute out of the congested area of St. Paul. In true Dumbo Willans tradition, he landed, boiling mad but safe, in the city dump. On this particular flight, balloon construction and flight operations were conducted by the Applied Science Division of Litton Industries, St. Paul, Minnesota. Nick had jumped from higher than that—up to 36,000 feet—during his training jumps at Lakewood Parachuting Center.

The next try was Strato-Jump II, made February 2, 1966, from Sioux Falls, South Dakota. Raven Industries of Sioux Falls built the balloon and handled the launch, tracking, and recovery operations. The balloon was constructed of ¾ mil polyethylene film, 340-feet long and 228-feet in diameter. At peak altitude, the helium-filled balloon contained a volume of five million cubic feet. Projected plans were for the balloon to reach between 120,000 feet and 122,000 feet. Nick actually got to 123,500 feet—the highest a man had ever been in a balloon. The gondola was a non-pressurized, expanded polystyrene enclosed cube, measuring 4 by 4 by 5½ feet. The frame was of welded tubular aluminum.

The balloon was not attached to the gondola, but rather to the apex of a 46-foot parachute. The parachute was then attached to the gondola. Engineers, ready for any emergency, figured the gondola could descend, with Piantanida in it, at a rate of twenty-five feet per second which is roughly equivalent to a landing in some of those older, "hot" modifications—hard, but tolerable. Nick weighed a solid 200 pounds to begin with, his equipment added another 160 pounds to give him a total of 360 pounds inside the gondola. Everything went off perfectly as Nick ascended to a record-breaking altitude.

The launch took place at 12:11 P.M. and, at 1:53, Nick reported his altimeter reading as 120,500 feet. Then he began his five-minute countdown to jump. At jump-minus-three, he reported putting his visor down and activating his G.E. oscillator (the transmitter used to record his rate of fall). At jump-minus-two, he released his seat belt, reset the gondola's automatic timer for another fifteen minutes (when it would automatically release itself from the balloon), and activated his oxygen bailout unit. At jump-minus-one, he tried to disconnect his main oxygen supply—his last link with the gondola before the jump. But the connection was frozen and with his heavy mittens, he could not manage to disconnect. He struggled for ten minutes trying to get the hose loose so he could make his long-dreamed-of jump. For lack of a suitable wrench, he simply could not get the fitting released.

He became almost frantic. He huffed and puffed, he cursed and prayed, but no matter how he tried, the main hose could not be disconnected.

Finally it became evident that he could not disconnect. If he struggled too hard and tore the hose loose, he would instantly lose the pressure from his suit. A loss of pressure at even *half* this altitude would be fatal. The blood would boil in his veins and he would explode. He had no choice now but to give up and ride back, still attached to his main oxygen supply and to the gondola.

Ed Yost of Raven Industries, the ground control director, notified Nick that they would give him a countdown and then release his gondola from the balloon. First, however, he must get seated and reconnect his seat belt. Nick couldn't fasten his seat belt because the heavy mittens made even a simple thing like that impossible. This became his greatest concern now, because without being fastened in the gondola, he could easily tumble out during the drop. Nick knew that the gondola would fall for several thousand feet before the parachute would inflate. And the gondola would probably be spinning and tumbling during the fall. The opening shock of the gondola's parachute would be extremely great. From the results of Kittinger's epic jump and other tests during that time, it was felt that a parachute opening at high speed and extremely high altitude would be beyond the survival capabilities of a human being. Nick was about to find out. He braced himself as best he could and hung on for dear life.

Yost gave the countdown and released the gondola at 2:12 P.M. from an altitude of 123,500 feet. For the next thirty-five seconds, the gondola hurtled faster and faster and Nick hung on, dreading the opening shock. If the gondola happened to be on its side with the open part down when the chute opened, Nick would be hurtled out. If he hurtled out, his oxygen hose would be ripped loose, his spacesuit would depressurize and he would die in seconds. His strength was dwindling rapidly. But for some reason, the gondola did not tumble or spin. It dropped stable as a rock for 25,500 feet. It reached a top speed of 600 mph or eighty percent of terminal velocity. At 98,000 feet the canopy caught air and inflated. Nick later said the opening was no more uncomfortable than a normal terminal velocity opening in free fall.

For the next thirty-one minutes, he rode the gondola down as it oscillated violently from side to side through strong upper winds. Periods of nausea overtook him as the gondola swung back and forth like a giant pendulum. Although he deactivated his reserve, he could not disarm his main canopy which was set to open at 6,500 feet. He wanted to bail out at a lower altitude but could not because he still could not get the oxygen hose loose. Realizing the landing would be hard, Jacques Istel radioed Nick to put his main chute under him and stand on it to help absorb the landing shock. At 2:45 he smashed into the ground. A hard, but safe landing.

Nick stayed in the gondola and finally pried the hose loose with a knife before the recovery crew reached him. Although the flight was a failure in terms of his jump, Nick proved two important facts: an object will not tumble or spin from high altitudes unless induced by some other force than just falling, and that the opening shock at high speed and high altitude is well within the limits of human endurance. The need for pressure suits that allow more maneuverability was obvious. More flexible gloves and suits would have to be developed. Three months later, Strato-Jump III began—early on the morning of May 6, 1966. Nick's wife, Janice, was there to wave to him and breathe a prayer for him as he lifted off and began the ascent.

Sixty minutes after launch, he had reached 57,000 feet. Over the intercom was heard a gush of air and a frantic, indistinguishable word, followed by a choked cry of "Emergency!" Instantly, the ground crew released the balloon and the gondola began the twenty-six minute descent with the unconscious Nick inside.

Apparently his face shield had blown out of the pressure suit. Later evidence indicated Nick had acted quickly to release his belt and tear loose connections in an attempt to dive over the side and reach life-sustaining air. If he had been only a few thousand feet higher his blood would have boiled and he would have died within seconds. As it was, he was without oxygen where unconsciousness occurs within a few seconds.

During the descent, Nick's flight surgeon flew nearby and landed moments before the gondola touched down. He was at Nick's side within thirty seconds. Nick was in a coma from oxygen starvation. At the hospital he was given oxygen in an attempt to restore his system, but the damage was irreparable. He was moved to other hospitals for more intensive care, but on August 29, 1966, almost four months after the attempt,

Nick Piantanida died without ever regaining consciousness. His courage and personal sacrifice will never be forgotten.

For a time, Hal Evans kept the project alive and planned to make the jump himself. He later dropped out as an active jumper and supported the efforts of Doug Angel and Frank Cordelle. They have scheduled their record attempt for the winter of 1971. A computer analysis will be made on all major aerodynamic parameters of the Stratospheric Free Fall Project. Again, Raven Industries will construct the balloon and David Clark Company will make the pressure suits. Among those supporting this project, in addition to Evans, are John Carlson, Cesar Aguilar, Ray Dobson, Bill Viets, Jeff Hoffman, and Bill Mehr.

5 AS THE PRO GOES
Professional Parachuting

Professional parachuting covers a lot of territory. To do more than scratch the surface is impossible in a brief space.

Without a doubt, Jim Hall and Dave Burt have earned a top position in the field. ParaVentures, with Burt as president and Hall as vice-president, operated a commercial sport parachuting center for nearly two years, staged exhibition-demonstration jumps, and promoted the sport greatly on the West Coast. They created the television series *Ripcord* and furnished the technical advice, jumpers, and equipment during the difficult development stages and through the first year. Unfortunately, the plots were created by non-jumping writers rather than parachutists. The stories were so highly contrived that impossible situations developed. Amazingly, many of these "impossible" stunts actually were accomplished.

In addition to the television show, ParaVentures made numerous television shorts and scenes to be used in other shows as well as motion pictures. Commercials for television and short films on parachuting kept them active. They grew from a two-man operation until they had eleven full-time employees and had outgrown their shoestring operation. With the development of the para-scuba program and "buddy-system" of free-fall training for military purposes, they decided to eliminate the sport parachuting operations and devote full time to professional parachuting services. With this new image, in 1963, they changed their organization to Parachuting Associates, Inc., with Burt and Hall exchanging positions as president and vice-president, and taking in a third, highly skilled professional, Bob Sinclair, as associate. Their Air Force training film *Passport to Safety* won numerous awards. In this film, top professionals Arthur "Bud" Kiesow (with more than a thousand jumps to his credit) and Ralph Weekly (one-time paratrooper company commander) doubled as the Air Force pilots throughout the film. Exciting and dramatic motion picture footage was filmed in free fall with helmet-mounted cameras on the free-falling cameraman. Free-fall photographer Bob Sinclair took on this demanding specialty. They went on to film commercials of every type—including one for Lilt showing Carol Penrod setting her hair with curlers while in free fall and one of another jumper loading Kodak's Instamatic camera and taking still shots of a fellow jumper. Among the television shows where their parachuting scenes were used were *Run For Your Life, 12 O'Clock High, Man From U.N.C.L.E., Voyage to the Bottom of the Sea, Kraft Theater,* and *Bob Hope's Chrysler Theater.* On one of his Hollywood trips, TV's Johnny Carson received his jump training and made his first jump, a sixty-second delayed free fall, with Bob Sinclair as his "buddy-system" partner. It was filmed in free fall and aired on NBC's *Tonight Show* in July, 1968.

Although Parachuting Associates, Inc., has top professionals and was the first to concentrate on the professional aspects beyond sport jumping, they do not have a monopoly in this field. For example, the *Ripcord* TV show went on to "better" things (the second season was in color) and to oblivion, at the hands of other professionals. The parachuting scenes were frequently concocted and unlikely, but everyone agreed they were different and interesting. If the actors and story had been as good as the parachuting photography and sequences, the show might have survived a little longer.

Parachuting Associates set the pace for excitement when a "student," Bob Sinclair doubling, got tangled in his static line during a training drop. The hero, Dave Burt doubling, slid down the line, cut the static line, and they fell away. Then the hero opened his student's parachute before opening his own—not really as impossible as it may sound to some, however. It had happened in October, 1960, when George Van Roosmalen got tangled in his static line on his fourth student-training jump. His jumpmaster, Alfred Coxall, slid down the static line which broke as he reached the student; Coxall pulled the student's reserve ripcord and then, after falling clear of him, pulled his own.

The new cameramen and jumpers of the *Ripcord* TV show were pushed to better things each week as the non-jumping writers came up with midair fist-fights, shoot-outs, and you-name-it. One of the most spectacular shows was not planned for in the script, so they used what they could, then wrote another show to use the unscheduled footage. Cliff Winters flew the hero's plane (Cessna 182) while Howard Curtis flew the villain's plane (L-13). The plot was for the hero, Lyle Cameron, to lower himself onto the tail of the villain's plane where he would be able to control the villain's craft. The pilot of the hero's plane would then radio the villain, telling him to land or the hero would force the plane into the ground. They tried it several times with sandbags to see if Curtis could keep control with the extra weight on the plane's tail—he could. Cameras were rolling as the scene began as planned. Winters maneuvered in behind and above Curtis' plane, and Cameron prepared to lower himself. When the two planes were only separated by a dozen feet or so, Cameron lowered himself onto the plane below. Then everything went wrong.

Cameron's weight upset the control causing the L-13 to nose-up and smash into the 182 above. Cameron released the plane as quickly as possible, but it was too late. Both planes began breaking up as Cameron fell clear. Both pilots were also highly skilled stunt parachutists, fortunately. Curtis fought for control of the plane, but as it rolled out of conrtol, he cut all switches, released his seat belt, and bailed out—striking the wingstrut. He was dazed slightly, but quickly recovered, stabilized, and then pulled. He saw Cameron descending safely and watched his disabled plane smash into the middle of a tomato patch.

Winters wasn't having such an easy time with the 182. He had refused to wear a parachute because it hampered his movements. Director Leon Benson had insisted on it for this scene, however, so Winters wore a QAC type chute until after takeoff. Once airborne, he unsnapped it from its D-rings and tossed it on the floor behind him, leaving him with only the harness. When the midair collision came, the plane fell out of control and Winters knew he had to get out. He released his seat belt, clawed his way into the back of the tumbling plane, grabbed the chute by its carrying strap and bailed out! While tumbling free through space (the crash came at 4,000 feet—twenty-six seconds separated him from the earth) he struggled to snap the parachute back on his harness. Later, Curtis praised Winters' feat, comparing it to changing a tire while the car is still moving. Winters hooked up and opened in time to save his life. Shortly afterward, he was killed when his stunt plane's engine failed in inverted flight during a slow roll for an airshow crowd.

Director of photography, Monroe Askins, filmed the entire smash-up and continued filming as long as there was anything to shoot. Because it cost them roughly $30,000, another script was written to make use of the special footage.

Another stunt called for a senator to leap from a disabled airplane, but without any parachute. The hero had to overtake him in free fall and catch him where they would come down on one chute. Leigh Hunt played the senator and dropped out wearing a gray flannel suit, complete with white shirt and tie. A 26 foot conical pack was sewn into the rear of his coat so it appeared he was chuteless. He wore no reserve, of course. Howard Curtis played the hero who made the catch. Hunt found that he fell too slowly without the added weight of his reserve so he had to wear skindiving weights. Swapping a reserve for lead is quite a switch!

Another time, Glenn White, playing the part of a girl, was to catch a box of cargo in midair and pull the broken static line to open the cargo chute. Lyle Cameron was the free-fall cameraman putting it on film. Glenn had trouble getting the box (full of sand), but finally succeeded. As Glenn opened, Lyle was in close filming the stunt so got a face full of Glenn's canopy. He went through it, re-modifying White's double-L in the process.

In one episode, Curtis played a dope-peddling villain that hero Hunt catches in midair. The hero and the villain have a midair fist-fight where the hero knocks the villain unconscious. Then he takes a pistol out of the unconscious villain's pocket before pulling the villain's ripcord, then his own. Lyle Cameron captured every second of it on film. Ironically, after all the narrow escapes, Lyle broke his arm one peaceful day when he fell from his camera-perch in a tree!

Don Molitor took over the camera. Doyle Fields also did free-fall motion picture coverage while Bob Buquor shot many exciting free-fall stills for publicity use. A few years later, with nearly a thousand safe jumps, Bob accidentally landed in the Pacific Ocean during some camera work and was drowned.

Certainly one of the closest calls of all came when the script called for the hero's main parachute to be ripped away and he had to resort to his reserve. Darrell Creighton did the camera work while standing on the top wing of a Stearman biplane piloted by Cameron. Howard Curtis almost became a dead hero as he gamely fought with the partial main (about a third had been removed to be sure it did not work) then deployed his reserve as the script called for. When the reserve malfunctioned with the streaming main, he was in for some thrills. He pulled on lines and did everything possible to make it untangle and catch air. It finally caught and inflated inside the partial main— at roughly a hundred feet above the ground.

Professional jumping requires risks and dangers that are avoidable in the sport of parachuting. However, the average person thinks of all parachute jumps about the same—a parachute jump is a parachute jump, they say. Rod Pack changed all that.

At 14,500 feet, Pack made his 534th parachute jump. The only thing unusual about his jump was the fact that he was making an intentional parachute jump without a parachute. He did it on New Year's Day, 1965. Talk about starting the year off with a bang!

Pack got interested in sport jumping after seeing a movie short on skydiving. He began jumping in October, 1961, and made 306 jumps his first year, probably a record for a twelve-month period. A part-time movie stuntman, he got the idea of pulling off a stunt so spectacular that movie makers would have to notice. Cliff Winters had made a parachute jump while in a straightjacket—he pulled the ripcord with his teeth. Somebody had commented that the only way to beat that was to jump without one. Pack decided to do just that, but he wanted to live to tell about it.

He made his first jump with Bob Allen and his first hook-up in relative work with Bob Buquor. He began practicing passing a standard 24-foot reserve parachute with Allen, but wore a main parachute as well. Each time he would catch up with Allen, take the reserve, and carefully snap it onto his special harness. After about a hundred practice jumps, Pack was ready for the real thing.

His harness was constructed so the D-rings would stand out instead of lying flat against the webbing. As an additional safety precaution, his harness was fitted with an extra strap with a strong snap on the end. If anything should go wrong (the reserve had slipped out of their hands once during a practice jump) and he should be without the chute, he would try to hook onto Allen's harness and both come down on Allen's main chute. Finally they were ready for the try.

He secured some financial backing through television and periodical contracts and hired two top-notch free-fall cameramen who also happened to be close jump buddies of his. Doyle Fields handled the motion pictures while Bob Buquor rigged himself up for the still shots.

Although they had planned for 15,000 feet, Pack directed the pilot to start in on the final run at 14,600 feet when everybody was getting numb from the cold. Allen did the spotting and gave Pack the nod when all was set. Pack signaled "go" and Allen dived out. Pack plunged out immediately after him, followed by cameramen Fields and Buquor.

To compensate for the lack of parachutes, Pack had weighted himself so he would fall at the same speed as during the practice jumps. As long as he was above Allen, he was still fairly sure of accomplishing the jump successfully—he could adjust his fall to speed up by pulling his arms and legs in or otherwise adjusting his body position. If he got below Allen he would be in trouble. He would have difficulty getting back "up" on Allen's level and Allen would have difficulty in getting down to Pack's level. Allen was holding the reserve by the cloth handles at each end and could do little maneuvering without risking the chance of losing the chute. Pack ate up 4,000 feet carefully moving into position to take the chute. He could have done it in much less, but had ample time and did not want to rush things. He had ninety seconds from the time he left the plane until he would strike the ground. That was the "ample time."

He carefully moved in and got a firm grip on the heavy cloth handle on the top of the reserve. Allen hung on, afraid Pack didn't have a good grip. Pack nodded he had it, and Allen reluctantly released his grip. Instantly the reserve shot up over Pack's head; the 125 mph wind almost pulled it from his hand but he hung on, hoping the handle would not pull out. Allen hovered close at hand, ready to rush in and share his harness if Pack should lose his grip. Continuing to film the episode, Fields and Buquor moved in closer, ready to dart in for the midair rescue if Allen were to fail. Pack pulled the chute back down and positioned it under him as he fell face down in a head-high attitude. Although he could not hear the snap, he watched carefully and concentrated on snapping both D-rings securely. A sense of relief came over him as the last snap was in place and he knew he was safe—providing he didn't have a malfunction of his one and only chute.

He released his grip on the chute as he scanned the sky for his three fellow-jumpers and flared out in a stable position. Because there was no tie-down on the chute, it swung up on the D-rings and crashed into his face. He grabbed it and pushed it back down, tumbling momentarily. In an effort to push the reserve back into position his hand accidentally dragged the rip-cord free and his chute caught air. He was not prepared for the opening shock, and his head and heels met somewhere behind him during the opening. He jubilantly drifted down for a soft landing in a plowed field.

He had done it! He had jumped without a parachute, picked

Larry Pennell and Ken Curtis starred in the now defunct *Ripcord* show. Although professional jumpers doubled for all the jumping stunts in the series, Curtis got the bug and made a jump for the fun of it. Most will recognize him more for his role in *Gunsmoke* as Festus Hagan.

Professional jumping demands the ultimate in skill and daring. Here the good guy (Leigh Hunt) charges after the gun-toting bad guy (Howard Curtis) as cameraman Doyle Fields dangles from the wingstrut to film the scene for the television show *Ripcord*. (*Ron Simmons,* Parachute *magazine*)

Television's Johnny Carson gets an assist from professional parachutist Bob Sinclair. Johnny's first jump was a 60-second delayed free fall alongside Bob. This buddy system of training was developed by Parachuting Associates to train Air Force crewmen in free-fall techniques. (*Parachuting Associates, Inc.*)

Professional cameraman Bob Sinclair shooting 35mm movie footage. Note the cloth extensions between elbows and waist to give added control. Because of the restricted movement and vision, he has mounted the ripcord pocket on his sleeve. (*Parachuting Associates, Inc.*)

The buddy system of free-fall parachute training is a drastic departure from the traditional method of training. Instead of making several static-line jumps with immediate openings, the student begins with 60-second delayed free falls from 12,500 feet. Here Bud Kiesow (left) keeps a tight grip on his student, Maj. Gen. Griffith who made three "buddy" jumps. Gen. Griffith is Deputy Inspector General for Safety for the USAF. (*Parachuting Associates, Inc.*)

Movie stuntman Rod Pack, seen here with his equipment, gained the attention he wanted when he became the first man to make an intentional parachute jump *without* any parachute. He picked one up from a friend on the way down and landed safely. (*Bob Buquor*)

Robert H. Buquor, aircraft mechanic, pilot, and professional jumper, was considered by most to be the best free-fall photographer of his time. Bob was chosen by Rod Pack to make free-fall shots of the chuteless jump and to act as backup man in case a midair rescue was necessary. On the ground, Bob presented the roll of exposed film to Pack and collected a fee of $1,800. Not bad for only one jump. With nearly 1,000 safe jumps, Bob accidently landed in the Pacific Ocean during some camera work and was drowned. This remarkable photo of Buquor was taken by another highly skilled free-fall photographer, Ralph White. (*Ralph White*)

Before Rod Pack made his notorious "chuteless jump," he logged more than a hundred relative jumps with Bob Allen who would later carry the necessary parachute. Here he flys formation with another jumper, Helen Lord, high over California. (*Bob Buquor*)

one up on the way down, and landed safely . . . a stunt that might be duplicated, but not surpassed. The repercussions of his stunt were inevitable.

The Federal Aviation Administration required that a person wear *two* parachutes for any premeditated jump—he didn't even wear *one!* The jumper isn't the only one to hang for infractions of FAA regulations; the pilot shares the responsibility and pilot Harry Haynes was called on the carpet, too. The legal outcome was never made public, but the representatives of the FAA made it clear they wanted to make an example of the jumper and the pilot to prevent any future stunts of the same nature. U.S. Attorney Manuel Real filed a civil federal court suit against Pack asking $3,000 punitive damages and $4,000 against pilot Haynes.

Rumors of Pack's next stunt spread like wildfire—some had a touch of truth, but some did not. Many said that the FAA had permanently grounded Pack from any future jumping from airplanes. So he began plans for parachuting from . . . an automobile? Yep. Nobody could prevent him from parachuting from an automobile. Plans called for him to drive the automobile out of the back of a C-130 some 15,000 feet above the Pacific Ocean. During the fall, explosive charges would blow the doors off. Then Pack would make a parachute jump *from the automobile.*

Actually, the FAA did not ground him at all, and he continued jumping until he broke his leg in three places (racing motorcycles, not parachuting). By the time he broke his leg, he had made an additional sixty-four parachute jumps since the chuteless drop, some three months earlier.

Another stunt rumored to be in Pack's planning involved dropping from the open cockpit of an inverted Stearman biplane, doing aerial maneuvers and finally dropping back into the open seat once more. This would seem more feasible in a glider or jet—something without a propeller to chop him into mincemeat. This brings to mind an accident along similar lines that Pack will surely want to think about if he actually attempts to go through with it.

In 1931, pilot Dimitrije Ljumovich's airplane seat belt broke at 8,000 feet as he was in the inverted position at the top of a proposed loop. Ljumovich dropped out, upside down, as his plane continued over in the arc to complete the loop in pilotless flight. At the bottom of the loop, the plane and Ljumovich met in midair where the propeller neatly severed his leg. He opened his parachute, tore strips of cloth from his flying suit, and tied a tourniquet around the bleeding stump during descent. He landed on his one leg and not only lived, he lived to fly again—with a wooden leg.

Johnny Findley of Bloomington, Indiana, is only a part-time professional jumper, but his experiences are typical. This writer "trained" Johnny back in pre-PCA basic safety rules days and sent him aloft in a two-place plane to spot for himself and make a free fall. He was cautioned to simply get clear of the plane and pull—we'd concentrate on stable delay later—like on the second or third jump! Johnny jumped from 2,500 feet, did a beautiful stable delay of ten seconds and opened. He experienced a minor malfunction of his main canopy (flat circular, no sleeve or bag), but elected to ride it into the ground rather than inconvenience his instructor, who repacked the chute, by opening the reserve. An expert at both scuba diving and spelunking, he frequently combines the two by exploring underwater caves. His daring is excelled only by his limitless energy. It is not uncommon for him to spend the entire night exploring caves (he doesn't want to waste the daylight) and the entire day parachuting, flying, scuba diving, or shooting the rapids of a flooded mountain stream.

In the summer of 1968, Johnny undertook another of his typically unique projects. He attempted to swim the Colorado River—not across it, but the length of it. Don't laugh, he swam fifty-three miles of it before cutting it short due to his companions giving out. I sympathize with them, having churned through several miles of swollen mountain rapids with him some years ago. In June, 1969, he made a second effort, but this time doing it alone. Again he was interrupted short of his goal, this time by local authorities. A guy in his forties, Johnny still has the energy and imagination of a teenager.

He survives on sandwiches because he doesn't like to waste time sitting down to eat a meal—he can eat a sandwich on the move! Obviously this leaves little time to hold down a routine job so he sometimes gives up his "regular" job (electronics research technician presently working on power packages for our spacecraft) and goes into business for himself. His wife, Bea, has learned to accept this rather unorthodox conduct. His three children can't keep up with him. Because he excels in everything he does, Johnny could be expected to be brash, overbearing, and cocky. Yet, he is the living example of humility, courtesy, and brotherly love. He's the kind of guy that would not only give you the shirt off his back, he'd offer his shoes and socks, too.

When Johnny found that he could make money by jumping out of airplanes, he turned professional—on his second or third jump. Unfortunately, promoters who advertise and publicize a jump usually expect to see a jump made regardless of the weather, so most of us who contract for an exhibition jump go ahead and make it even at the risk of serious injury. Johnny is no exception.

He had seven years' experience when he prepared for these three "pay" jumps on Armed Forces Day. He knew the winds were too high, but he wouldn't cancel out. The first two downwind landings were rough. The third was a typical "crash and burn" type landing that left him in the hospital for half a year, wearing plaster pants up to his armpits. He had to come in downwind to clear some obstacles and just as he was about to land, a gust of wind caught his canopy and lead him into the ground—both hitting about the same time. Winds are probably the greatest threat to jumpers, but the spectators don't know that.

On a night jump Johnny staged, his plans called for all the lights at the fairgrounds to be turned off by a single master switch just prior to his jump. He fell with flares, tracing a beautiful trail across the sky like a giant meteor. When he opened up, the lights were to be turned back on, but nothing happened. A single spotlight from the grounds shined upward to mark the fairgrounds from the air and to illuminate the open canopy during descent. It was placed among tents and rides and trapeze and was not marking the landing area. Without the other lights on to illuminate the landing area, it only made matters worse, blinding him in the darkness. He descended over a huge black fairground knowing that every conceivable hazard lay beneath him. A normal jumper would have yelled and screamed for lights and cursed the man who was supposed to turn the master switch back on. To my knowledge, Johnny has never said a curse word—his most likely comment would have been, "By golly! Wish somebody'd turn the lights back on." He had no idea when he would hit, then he did. He struck the outside edge of the banked racetrack, his left leg taking all the force before his right leg touched down. His leg broke and he tumbled down the embankment, tangled in his chute in the darkness.

Finally the lights came on and eventually the man who was to control the lights came running up. Showing just a tinge of displeasure and pain as he lay there, Johnny asked the man why he had failed to turn the lights back on at the designated time. The attendant said he was so excited and engrossed watching the free fall and canopy descent that he just plain forgot all about it. Johnny was in the hospital three months for that jump. He learned the hard way that he should have had a fellow jumper who knew the operations to act as ground safety man and operate the lights.

Every jumper who has done very many professional jumps experiences unique situations that cannot be anticipated. I remember making an exhibition jump with my partner, Jim Thompson. We were descending into a county fair one Saturday afternoon when blasting commenced in the quarry adjoining the vacant field. We hung helplessly like clay pigeons, waiting to be literally shot out of the saddle by flying rocks. Another time, I was descending into an extremely tight area in front of the outdoor stage facing the grandstand at a county fair. A sudden and violent squall swept the area. I looked down to see the backdrop and parts of the stage blow away along with some of the tents. Although I had hit the target on the first jump, on this one I hitchhiked back from nearly a mile downwind of the fairgrounds.

Although the Santa Claus jumps are becoming less frequent —coming in by helicopter is more positive—they still thrill the kids and parents alike. Unfortunately, several deaths have occurred during Santa Claus jumps. Because of the bad weather over most of the country during the winter, "Santas" parachuting in have been blown into rivers and drowned, or into powerlines and electrocuted. Children tend to cry if they see Santa Claus electrocuted right before their bright little eyes.

Even if Santa doesn't drift off into the surrounding countryside or get killed, he may break his ankle like Charles Barnes did at Panama City. The children's shouts of glee gave way to murmurs of concern as Santa moaned and groaned and writhed on the ground, holding his ankle. A stand-in Santa slipped under the parachute's folds with Barnes and switched into the Santa costume. The stand-in Santa walked away with all the children happily trotting after him. When most of the children were gone, ambulance attendants dragged Barnes out from under the parachute and took him to the hospital for treatment.

Santa jumps go back as far as December, 1912, when a Captain Penfold arranged the jump with a chocolate company. Wearing the outfit of "Father Christmas," he ascended to 3,000 feet in a balloon and floated down in a parachute. When he landed, he passed out chocolate candy to the local children.

Pictured here is professional parachutist Kaz Ostrom, the "Viking of the Sky," making a Santa Claus jump into a shopping center. This photo was made during a jump for Christmas, 1962, before the development of the more popular sport parachutes. However, even with this modification (5-TU) Kaz is turning in a top-notch, professional performance. He began his jumping career in Fort Benning, Georgia, in 1957. He went on to the 77th Special Forces Group (Guerrilla warfare) at Fort Bragg, North Carolina, for night drops onto unlighted drop zones. Then in September, 1958, he found himself a part of the first guinea-pig outfit to take part in Project HALO (High Altitude-Low Opening). Kaz did more jumping than the average paratrooper. When he was discharged, he had 119 military jumps —ninety-eight of them free falls.

With some valuable parachuting experience and no money, Kaz decided to turn "pro." His first jump was as Harvey, the world's largest Easter Bunny. He parachuted into a shopping center and an exciting career as a professional parachutist. But even the top jumpers can't win them all—not doing exhibition jumps into shopping centers and fairs and racetracks. Sooner or later it was bound to happen, and it did in July, 1963. A

Professional parachutist Kaz Ostrom making a Santa Claus jump into a shopping center. Using a five-gore separation TU Modification, he's doing all right. (*Dennis Galloway*)

Johnny Finley is seen on a typical, hazardous, professional demonstration. He shot over powerlines and buildings in a 22-knot wind to land right on the target—placed in the middle of a street! Note the two pilot chutes for more positive openings. Since this photo was taken, Johnny has begun flying the new wing designs, something to compete with those winds.

For a professional to survive in today's field of experts, he must not only land on the target, he also must use modern multi-colored sport canopies and carry smoke. Powerlines, lights, stands, and other hazardous obstacles distinguish this exhibition jump from sport parachuting where safety rules apply. (*Joe Gonzales, U.S. Army*)

Professional jumping often requires special equipment or aircraft. When the author had to make three successive water jumps during an afternoon watershow, he called on his friend and fellow pilot, Nashville candy executive D. C. Lovelace. Here, with Lovelace at the controls of his floatplane, the author makes a dry-run, test drop. (*George Green*)

With Stone Mountain looming behind tall Georgia pines, one of
the thirty-eight contestants at the Stone Mountain Meet drops into
the target. This was the first of the big-money meets that set the
pace. Bob Holler walked off with the $1,000 first prize money.

Interested Las Vegas spectators
help Steve Snyder sort his canopy
from the sagebrush. He was one
of the dozens who made a mass
drop into the vacant lot across
from the Thunderbird Hotel, host
for the first National Professional
Parachuting Championships.

gust of wind and a turn just off the ground resulted in a violent oscillation. Kaz's left leg caught all the weight as he swung into the ground, snapping five tendons and putting him out of the jumping game. Like men in any other occupation who get paid well for taking risks, the professional parachutist has to be willing to pay the price himself, too.

Because there are so many enthusiastic sport jumpers who are willing to jump for glory instead of money, the professional parachutist frequently finds himself losing out at airshows, county fairs, and other special celebrations. A few years ago a jumper could expect to make no less than one hundred dollars per jump—a jump-and-pull from 2,500 feet. But as more and more skilled jumpers became available, the price decreased and the performance improved (good old American competition?). Without an ironclad contract, the professional jumper could expect himself to be put out of the running by local clubs or individuals who would jump for much less—frequently for cost of the plane rental only. Instead of a jump-and-pull from 2,500 feet, the sponsor could now expect (and get) multiple jumps with different colored smoke from the jump plane and jumpers; triple baton passes with interlacing smoke of red, white, and blue; and pinpoint accuracy in multi-colored, specially manufactured sport parachutes—all for only the cost of gas and oil on the jump plane! For $25 the sponsor gets what he would have paid $300 for a few years earlier. With this sort of competition between individuals and local clubs, the professional has to be satisfied with being a part-time parachutist and hold a steady job on the ground the rest of the time.

Very few of the thousands of free-fall parachutists in the United States can make a living solely by parachuting from airplanes, but as competition jumping offers bigger and better prizes—large sums of cash instead of an eight-dollar trophy—chances for a sport jumper to turn pro increase. A few years ago a prize as valuable as a complete parachute pack for first place was considered fantastic. Now it is not unusual for a local club to award a cash prize of $500 for first place and slightly less for second and third place winners. Larger clubs or groups may offer $1,000 or more. As more and more meets are scheduled, top jumpers can follow the circuit to take part in money-making events.

In May, 1965, the Georgia Skydivers hosted a meet at Stone Mountain, Georgia, that attracted jumpers from all across the country. First prize was $1,000 cash with other prizes totaling an additional $700 cash. This was the first of big "money meets" in the nation and it set the pace. The Stone Mountain Meet was also the first major meet to use the 5 x 5 scoring system—anything outside five meters was not measured or scored. However, this didn't matter much because competitor Bill Finch of Charleston, South Carolina, had an average of less than one meter on his four accuracy jumps. Bob Holler of Hyattville, Maryland, however, averaged better overall and took the $1,000 prize money.

That same month, another money meet was held at Taft, California, and forty jumpers entered the Taft Grand Prix in hopes of winning some of more than $1,000 in cash prizes. Daryl Henry took top place at that meet.

With meets like these, the chances of a top sport jumper turning pro improved greatly. Hal Evans, promoter extraordinary, convinced the right people that the time was ripe for the first National Professional Parachuting Championship and convention. It was hosted by the Hotel Thunderbird, Las Vegas, Nevada. This was the gathering point for forty-two of the best known, top jumpers from across the country. Paul "Pop" Poppenhager and Gary Dupris came all the way from Florida; Tim Saltonstall and Maxine Hartman came from New York; Susie Clements and Jeanni McCombs represented California along with husband-and-wife jumpers Frank and Marilyn Hutchins; Daryl Henry and Bob Hill came down from Canada to participate. Others participating as judges, pilots, or coordinators, included Phil Miller, Mr. and Mrs. Lyle Cameron, and Mr. and Mrs. Steve Snyder. And as an extra attraction, Loy Brydon led his crew of Golden Knights on some exhibition-demonstration jumps.

The Thunderbird spared nothing to make the jumpers welcome and happy in Las Vegas. For the $100 entry fee, each jumper received eight days' stay at the Thunderbird in luxurious air-conditioned rooms, king-size beds, meals, all parachute jumps—both competition and fun jumps—and a closing banquet featuring Jack Benny.

At the end of the meet, Chuck Yeager presented a $2,000

check to Bob Holler and a $1,000 check to Billy Lockward. This is the same Bob Holler who had pocketed $1,000 at Stone Mountain only a month earlier. Another $1,000 was given away in a drawing among the contestants. Professional jumping, at least on a part-time basis, was now within the grasp of the weekend sport jumper.

MILITARY

Before leaving the general area of exhibition-demonstration-professional jumping, special mention should be paid to the various military teams. Although there are teams and clubs and individuals representing virtually every branch of our military services, the United States Army Parachute Team must be recognized as the leader. This is not to say that some of the Army teams have never lost competitions to some of the other service teams, such as the jump-off with the Marine team in June, 1965. The Army was the first to not only allow, but to actually encourage, free-fall parachuting activities. In April, 1958, it issued authorization and got a head start on the other services. The Navy followed in September, 1960, with approval of the United States Navy Parachute Exhibition Team which became "The Chuting Stars." However, it wasn't until January, 1962, that the Navy issued SECNAV Instruction 1700.6C that actually authorized and encouraged participation of Navy and Marine Corps personnel in free-fall parachuting.

In 1959, Jacques Istel had managed to get through to General Curtis LeMay and sold the idea of sport jumping to the Air Force. Shortly after, a message went out to all commands stating that the local base commander could authorize his men to jump, provided they were a club sanctioned by PCA. The only trouble there was that the majority of base commanders would not do so. Since they had a choice, they took the status quo attitude. In 1962, the USAF in Europe published regulation 215-3 that opened the door wider and allowed many Air Force clubs to develop. Soon a part-time demonstration team called "The Blue Masters" began to represent the Air Force in exhibition jumps in Europe and bordering countries. In 1964, a PCA-backed effort to get parachuting approved for Air Force personnel without their base commander's permission was submitted and officially rejected. However, through the diligent work of a handful of dedicated Air Force men, sport parachuting was added to the curriculum of the Air Force Academy.

In 1964, Major John Garrity, Captain Craig Elliot, Sergeant James Howell, and Sergeant Morton Freedman were temporarily assigned to the academy to set up a cadet parachute club, train jumpmasters, and establish operating procedures. Later, Major Garrity, Sergeant Freedman, and Sergeant Vernon Morgan were assigned on permanent basis to conduct two credit-earning courses. Although the cadet could earn semester hours, the course was strictly voluntary.

Parachuting 490 became the basic course in parachuting and included some 37 hours of ground training plus ten free-fall jumps; parachuting 491 was a jumpmaster course with 46 hours of classes plus fifteen additional jumps. There is also a cadet parachute team for weekend jumping on a non-credit basis and a twelve-man competition team that meets against other colleges and universities. In selling the idea of parachuting courses, OIC Major Garrity said, "We feel that no other activity, short of combat, offers us a greater opportunity to ingrain into the future officers, the indelible character of aggressiveness, self-discipline, responsibility, leadership, esprit de corps, and manhood. These courses are not just 'sport jumping,' but teach techniques of HALO, emergency bailout, and familiarity with techniques used by our professional parachutists." Although Major Garrity, his fellow officers, and NCO's have been assigned tours of duty in Vietnam, they have alternated tours so at least several of the original staff are always at the Academy.

There are other Air Force parachutists—all relatively small groups when compared to the Army's thousands—and all are specialists in their trade. The Air Rescue Service is one of the oldest groups. With their motto, "That Others May Live," these paramedics and pararescue men circle the globe, performing yeomen service by snatching people back from the grave.

Victims of air crashes, boat sinkings, floods, earthquakes, and other natural or man-made disasters represent some of those saved by the pararescue team. These hardy jumpers are trained medical technicians, ready to parachute into all types of situations to sustain life. Evan Hale of Gladstone, Oregon, is typical of the outfit. A former regional director of PCA as well as a reservist and paramedic, Hale has saved many lives by parachuting into crash sites and performing minor surgery, setting bones, and comforting victims until ground rescue parties can reach the scene.

Space doesn't permit extensive coverage of this vital work of the many miracles performed by these men but without any doubt, the pararescue jumpers are among the most skilled professionals of any service. With the advent of the space age the role of the pararescue team increased to include scuba training. Teams of parascuba men are ready to parachute into any waters to recover astronauts, who through some emergency situation, are forced down outside the prime recovery areas where Navy frogmen teams normally come in by helicopter to perform this function.

Another relatively small group of Air Force parachutists is the Combat Control team. These men are air traffic controllers who have the unpleasant job of jumping in ahead of the main airborne troops. Once on the ground, they set up drop zone and landing zone aids, direct paradrops of men and equipment, and control the air traffic in and out of the fighting area. Often found side by side with the combat controllers are the combat weather teams whose mission is to assist in the airborne invasion with up-to-date meteorological data.

There may even be a 1,500 mph jet jockey jumping in the same load with his army paratroop friends. His unique role is to direct air strikes in support of the ground troops. Through this Forward Air Controller's flying and jump training, he knows both the Army and Air Force problems, limitations, and capabilities, thereby giving vital air strike assistance to the ground forces.

And there are others—each a small but vital unit—the Air Force Intelligence teams, survival technicians, Air Force liaison officers with the Army airborne units, and the Air Commandos (the counter-insurgency unit).

When the Army approved and encouraged parachuting for sport in 1958, clubs were quickly formed at Fort Campbell, Kentucky, and Fort Bragg, North Carolina, training bases of the Army Airborne troops. Although the United States Army Parachute Team (USAPT) based at Fort Bragg has been instrumental in developing and testing new equipment and techniques, its main function has been one of public relations.

In February, 1964, the team was authorized forty-two enlisted men and seven officers plus three officer-pilots and two flight engineers. They were divided into three teams: the competition team, the black demonstration team, and the gold demonstration team. Research and testing are conducted by parachutists from any of the three teams. Selection to the USAPT is a feather in the cap of any parachutist because qualifications are high and the number who can be accepted are few; vacancies are filled as each member completes his tour of duty with the team. For several years, at every major international parachute competition, the American team was dominated by members of the U.S. Army Parachute Team and, even before the team was officially formed, by members of the airborne.

Early competition jumpers from the Army, such as Loy Brydon, Danny Byard, and Curt Hughes, were instrumental in designing, testing, and manufacturing parachutes with modifications of much higher performance than the renowned blank gore parachute. Forming a company called Capital Parachuting Enterprises, the three designed and hold patents on the Double-L, Single-T, Double-T, and TU modifications. These were the winning chutes at every major parachute competition until the development of sport chutes like the Para-Commander and Cross-Bow. Although the TU modification had a high rate of descent, it also had the most forward speed. Dead-center landings were difficult, but men like Dick Fortenberry and Loy Brydon made them look easy. This modification was very unforgiving of mistakes, however, and many a jumper has been wiped out temporarily by turning too close to the ground.

The many military parachuting activities are so diversified, it is difficult to adequately discuss each one individually. Certainly the uses of the parachute by the Special Forces (Green Beret) in unconventional warfare must be briefly mentioned. They have held the major role in the development of project HALO.

The conventional way of getting airborne troops into a given area is by helicopter or by large troop-carriers. Both must come in over the enemy territory at low altitude and make enough noise to wake the dead. In the parachute operations from troop carriers, hundreds of airborne troops are dumped

Members of the Air Rescue Service have saved hundreds of lives all around the world. Jumping with scuba gear is an exacting art. Sgt. Nicolas Klimis, pararescue supervisor, checks the equipment of Sgt. Joe Williams prior to a training jump into the Gulf of Mexico. (*U.S. Air Force*)

Mass drops of airborne troops are becoming a thing of the past as helicopter assaults are more suitable to modern warfare. For special, behind-the-line guerrilla operations, HALO specialists are called in. (*U.S. Air Force*)

Training for HALO operations, two of the Army's Special Forces members begin their two-minute free fall. The Air Force and Navy also have training in HALO techniques. Contrast this with the traditional mass drops from low-flying troop carriers. (*U.S. Army*)

The MC-1 HALO parachute is large enough to allow the specialist to carry more than a hundred pounds of additional equipment for special guerrilla warfare assignments. Unlike conventional troop parachutes, it is steerable. (*Air Force Academy*)

into the sky. Parachutes are automatically opened by static lines at a thousand feet or so and the soldier drifts down, completely at the mercy of the enemy's ground fire, and there is enemy fire if there is an enemy within five miles of the drop zone. An enemy would have to be deaf not to hear the planes at such a low altitude and would have to be blind not to see the sky darkened by hundreds of parachutes. If the planes come in over the territory at a higher altitude, the jumpers are simply drifting down that much longer and can drift that much farther from the intended drop zone. Project HALO eliminates these hazards.

Highly specialized teams—expert free-fall parachutists specializing in demolitions, communications, weapons, or medicine—exit a relatively small, single-engine plane flying some 20,000 feet above their objective. The plane is too high to be heard or seen. Carrying large quantities of explosives and other necessary equipment, the team free falls, using skydiving techniques to maintain stability and to glide to the proper opening point, down to very low altitudes where they deploy the chutes and land immediately. Unless an enemy is almost on the landing spot of the individual HALO jumper, the jump will go undetected.

Several highly specialized teams may be dropped into the area at one time—each with some specific objective such as a bridge, dam, power plant, or other vital facility. A dozen skilled specialists—whose arrival and presence is unknown to the enemy—can do more damage with less risk than several hundred regular paratroopers who have alerted the entire countryside with a traditional mass drop. This doesn't mean that there are not still occasions when sheer masses are necessary, of course, but for special guerrilla-type assignments, the HALO specialists are the answer. The Navy's SEAL teams (Sea, Air, Land) specialize in unconventional warfare which also includes parachuting activities.

SMOKEJUMPERS

Although the concept of fighting an enemy through the use of aerial drops of men and supplies goes back to Ben Franklin, the practical aspects of this type warfare were actually ironed out by a handful of determined and dedicated men who adopted the idea to fight fires, not wars.

From shortly after World War I until 1939 there had been some meager attempts to use aircraft both for spotting fires and for bombing them with water and chemicals. In 1939, the bombing experiments were given up in favor of an experiment which included the dropping of firefighters, as well as equipment, by parachute. The Eagle Parachute Company of Lancaster, Pennsylvania, got the contract to furnish the equipment and jumpers for the experiment. Their training outfit consisted of an Eagle 30-foot main backpack chute and a 27-foot reserve chute. Eagle also manufactured a felt-padded suit that would protect the jumper from tree landings or unusually rough terrain. Frank M. Derry was in charge of the small group of professional jumpers who participated.

The experiment proved that aerial firefighters, smokejumpers, could effectively reduce loss of valuable forests. The first year of operation the smokejumpers earned their keep by saving an estimated $30,000 worth of timberland. Watching the training and operations were four Army staff officers. One officer was Major William Cary Lee, who later became first Chief of the Airborne Command and father of United States airborne doctrine. He adapted forest service techniques in organizing the first paratroop training base at Fort Benning, Georgia. Although the idea of aerial delivery of men was conceived as a military concept, it took the dedicated men of the forest service to prove it would work. Meanwhile, in Europe, Germany's airborne troops were achieving victories on every front.

Each summer the smokejumper schools are swamped by college men who learn firefighting and parachuting. The rugged training and conditioning received by the smokejumper trainee is comparable to the military's program. A raging fire can be just as deadly as any enemy soldier and more than one smokejumper has lost his life to the flames. A branch of the Department of Agriculture, the Forest Service maintains several bases for the smokejumper operations. However, the school and headquarters at Missoula, Montana, is the largest and best known.

The forest service also has the edge on the Air Force's paramedic operations, having made the first rescue jumps back in

Millions of dollars worth of timber have been saved since the parachute came into use as a firefighting weapon of the Forest Service. Two smokejumpers wait in the door as the jumpmaster "spots" for them. (*Burr Saterfield*)

Static lines deploy the chutes of these smokejumpers who exit over rough terrain. Tree landings are common, obviously. (*Burr Saterfield*)

1940. That year smokejumper Chester N. Derry and Dr. Leo P. Martin parachuted into the Bitterroot Forest to aid victims of a plane crash. Although some pararescue work is still done by smokejumpers, the Air Force teams usually handle this type of work now; their search-rescue operations are highly organized and their paramedics are specially trained.

These, then, are just some of the uses of the parachute and a brief account of the men who jump. Some jump to save their own lives—emergency; some jump to save the lives of others —testing and rescue. A few jump for money—exhibition, others jump for their country—military. But probably the greatest number jump for no other reason than just because it's fun. Parachuting for sport is difficult for the non-jumper to understand. All the other types of parachuting seem to have some logical and practical reason behind them. But jumping into space thousands of feet above the ground just for the fun of it?

6 SOARING WITHOUT WINGS
Free-Fall Parachuting

At one time there were only two types of parachuting: *free-fall* parachuting where the jumper activates his own parachute by pulling a ripcord, and *static-line* jumping where the parachute is automatically opened by a line attached to the aircraft on one end and to the parachute pack on the other.

This is still basically true and a jumper will normally log his jumps as a free-fall jump or a static-line jump. An example of free-fall jumping is the emergency jump when a pilot bails out and pulls his ripcord. An example of a static-line jump is the paratrooper who takes part in mass drops in military operations. Another example of static-line deployed parachutes is cargo dropping by parachute. Obviously a crate of ammunitions cannot pull a ripcord, so the static line does the job.

More and more *automatic openers* are being used in all phases of parachute operations now, so this might be considered a third category. Most emergency jumps (actually nowadays these are usually ejections rather than jumps) are made with automatic openers. These openers are operated either by a timer or by barometric pressure and activate the parachute with a spring or explosive charge. There are a number of automatic openers available to the sport jumper, too. These are intended to operate as backup systems to activate the main or the reserve parachute, if the jumper fails to activate the parachute himself. Certainly the sport parachuting world owes a great deal to Steve Snyder for developing several automatic openers used extensively in sport parachuting. This writer can personally vouch for Snyder's reserve opener, having used it for several years. Snyder's files contain a number of letters from grateful persons who had their lives saved by his opener. For developing the reserve opener, Snyder was awarded the Leo Stevens medal, parachuting's highest award.

Free-fall parachuting itself should be divided into two categories: *controlled* free fall and *uncontrolled* free fall. A turn or a backloop may indicate skill on the part of one jumper and be considered uncontrolled free fall on the part of another—the only difference being *intent,* not the maneuver itself. A beginning free-fall jumper will make many turns before he learns to do one intentionally. The fact that a student made two right turns and a backloop is not very impressive if he was still hooked to his static line at the time!

In early training jumps—with the chute deployed by a static line—the jumper will be concentrating on stability for the three or four seconds before his parachute is completely inflated. The instructor will be watching to see that the jumper learns to assume the basic stable spread position and hold it while the chute inflates, then that he can remain stable while he reaches in and pulls a dummy ripcord. Finally after half a dozen or so static-line jumps, the instructor will allow his student to begin short free falls—probably no more than three to five seconds at first. Then he will move up to ten second delays and the fun will begin.

Charts A & B show the distance and the speed in feet per second during free fall. Within four seconds the jumper is falling faster than one hundred feet per second, and, during the next eight seconds, he accelerates an additional seventy feet per second. Within four seconds a jumper is falling at more than 50 percent of his maximum speed! During the jump, the first four or five seconds are the only ones in which a jumper really senses that he is falling. The position of the body will determine the sensations. In the prone, face-to-earth position, there is little sensation of falling. But in the head-high, standing position, a jumper may experience the elevator effect momentarily, particularly if he looks up at the plane as it appears to rush away from him.

Chart A   Distance Fallen In Free-Fall Stable Spread Position

Seconds	Distance	Seconds	Distance	Seconds	Distance	Seconds	Distance
1	16	16	2179	31	4789	46	7399
2	62	17	2353	32	4963	47	7573
3	138	18	2527	33	5137	48	7747
4	242	19	2701	34	5311	49	7921
5	366	20	2875	35	5485	50	8095
6	504	21	3049	36	5659	51	8269
7	652	22	3223	37	5833	52	8443
8	808	23	3397	38	6007	53	8617
9	971	24	3571	39	6181	54	8791
10	1138	25	3745	40	6355	55	8965
11	1309	26	3919	41	6529	56	9139
12	1483	27	4093	42	6703	57	9313
13	1657	28	4267	43	6877	58	9487
14	1831	29	4441	44	7051	59	9661
15	2005	30	4615	45	7225	60	9835

Chart B   Distance Fallen Each Second to Terminal Velocity

Seconds	Distance
1	16
2	46
3	76
4	104
5	124
6	138
7	148
8	156
9	163
10	167
11	171
12	174

(Courtesy of Parachutes, Inc.)

As the parachutist drops away from the jump plane in a basic spread position (which may be a rigid spread-eagle or a relaxed French frog position) he becomes aware of the sudden silence that envelopes him—the sense of detachment that makes him feel more like an observer than a participant. He feels a strong wind blowing up from below and senses that he is accelerating even though the ground remains motionless, distant, and of no concern up here in this other world.

Remaining in the stable spread position, he feels his body slowing down as he approaches terminal velocity of 174 feet per second—roughly 120 mph. From all outward sensations he has now ceased to fall and he feels that he is floating in a strong wind . . . which is about what he is doing. Although still plummeting toward the earth at 174 feet per second, he no

Look ma, no hands! Automatic openers are being used more and more in sport jumping by both students and experts. Here the jumper maintains a stable spread position while his automatic opener releases his backpack. The sleeve appears too small for the canopy as it "slumps." The automatic openers are also available for the emergency chute. (*Ralph White*)

Static-line jumps usually precede free-fall training. Here student Bill Floyd of Chattanooga makes his first static-line jump under the watchful eyes of the author who was his instructor-jumpmaster. The static line will release the student's parachute roughly ten feet below the plane.

This is the jumpmaster's view of a student's actions during his first static-line jump. This particular jumper is instinctively running in place and clutching his reserve. He quickly recovered his wits and assumed a basic stable spread position before the static line released his pilot chute.

Even a novice might guess that this jumper is assuming the more relaxed frog position. Gloves are more for control than warmth, giving a larger surface for the hands. Rate of descent will be slightly faster than in the basic stable spread position. (*Ralph White*)

The basic stable spread position affords the slowest rate of free fall. This jumper appears to be on final approach to runway 6. (*Ralph White*)

The relaxed frog position allows greater freedom of movement and is preferred by virtually everyone who has first learned to maintain a basic spread. Ken Rounds demonstrates. By extending his legs slightly and leaving his hands in the present position, he can move forward. By extending his arms slightly and drawing the feet back, he will slide backward. Twisting his hands or extending one leg in the present position will initiate a turn. (*Ralph White*)

hese six jumpers illustrate an assortment of positions. The three jumpers in the
nter have "hooked up" while the other three are adjusting their fall to intercept
d form a six-man star. The jumper on the left is working from a stable spread,
oving his arms back slightly to move forward and downward. The jumper second
om left has thrown on the brakes in an effort to keep from overshooting or getting
to the captured air (less dense) caused by jumpers below. He will tighten up to
crease his rate of fall and join the three below. At right, the jumper is extending
s legs and pulling his arms back to glide forward. The positions of his hands indi-
ate he may be attempting to "swim" forward—actually he is holding them firm so
ey deflect the air backward and pull him forward. (*Bob Buquor*)

longer feels the pull of gravity because it is equalized by the
wind resistance against his body. He is balanced precariously
on a huge column of air that has piled up beneath him, and
the slightest off-balance movement will now throw him into a
spin, backloop, barrel roll, or other unstable fall. Until a
jumper gains experience, he must continue to concentrate on
maintaining stability—no fancy aerobatics yet.

As progress is made to longer delays, the free-fall parachutist
quickly learns that the stable spread position is more difficult to
maintain after terminal velocity is reached than it is at the slower
speeds. The rigid spread-eagle position used in the earlier static-
line training jumps will now result in constant buffetting, pitching, and yawing. Now is the time to relax into the French frog
position with the legs bent and the arms bent so the hands are
comfortably near the shoulders (see illustration). In the French
frog position the rate of descent is greater than in the basic

spread position. Control is more precarious now because the body is drawn up into a smaller area. In the event the jumper suddenly finds himself inverted (it's likely he will on the early attempts) and looking up at the sky instead of down at the ground, the remedial action is simply arch back and spread arms and legs back to the basic stable spread. Within a second or two he will be back in the face-to-earth position and stable . . . and can try again.

The basic spread-eagle position with the arched back is the answer to any uncontrolled fall and will result in instant recovery to the face-to-earth position. The only possible exception is the flat spin that is difficult to stop, but easy to avoid. When a free-fall jumper feels himself turning to one side or the other, he must immediately twist his body to counter it. The hands, feet, trunk, and head can all be employed either to initiate a turn or to stop it. If a spin becomes fast and the jumper cannot otherwise counter it, he sweeps his arms back to the sides and bends forward at the waist. This will cause a forward tumble and break the flow of air that is supporting the spin. After a tumble or two, the back is arched and the arms and legs thrown out in the basic spread position. Almost instantly the jumper will be stable in a face-to-earth position. It is best to avoid letting any turns develop into spins.

Once the student jumper has learned to maintain stability and to recover from uncontrolled free fall, he can begin concentrating on free-fall maneuvers. After some experience he will find himself making turns and loops and rolls without any conscious effort at all. Although he will be employing various techniques, they will be done as effortlessly as when turning around on the ground—actually easier. To explain in words how to maintain stability and how to execute turns is something like trying to explain how to balance and steer a bicycle when the person has never even been on a bicycle. There are certain basics to know, but from then on, it's a matter of doing it until it becomes second nature.

There are two main points for the jumper to keep in mind when learning aerobatics: (1) establish a reference point on the ground and use it to maintain a firm heading and (2) start from a flat, stable position with the horizon comfortably visible to the front. With these two references determined before he begins, the jumper can accomplish precision turns, loops, and rolls, and always end the maneuver exactly where he began. It is imperative that he keep his eyes open and not lose sight of reference points more than is necessary. Obviously, if he doesn't know where he is when he starts a maneuver, he has no way of knowing when he has finished it, either.

TURNS

Basically there are three types of turns: *hand* turns, *foot* turns, and *body* turns. However, any accomplished jumper will employ combinations of these and come up with some unique ideas of his own.

It was once thought there were *only* these three basic turns. Later modifications of these turns included the arms and legs. Then the hand turn was supplemented by the push turn which combined with the arms and body until virtually every part of the body is now employed in making such fast turns that judging is nearly impossible. To the untrained eye, some of the champion-style (free-fall maneuvering) jumpers appear to be tumbling and spinning in totally uncontrolled fall. In reality, they are making precision 360-degree turns to the right and left with backloops . . . in roughly seven seconds! By drawing the body up into a tight button-like position, turns can be executed with lightning speed.

The story persists that Loy Brydon, on a competition-style jump, removed his helmet in free fall and simply swung it from his head to his rear and back a couple of times. In the tight position it appeared to the judges on the ground that he had completed his series of turns and loops in record-breaking time. Brydon will neither deny nor confirm the story. However anybody who has tried to judge a style event—even using modern optics—finds the story quite feasible.

Hand turns are always done from the French frog position where the body offers a minimum of resistance and can easily spin about its axis or center of gravity. To execute a hand turn to the right, for example, the hands remain pointed straight ahead, but are tilted at a 45-degree angle so the heel of the right hand is down and the heel of the left hand is up. To

Stable openings are not only safer, they are more comfortable than an uncontrolled opening. Illustrated here the jumper has checked to be sure he has the ripcord handle (and not another part of harness hardware) in his hand, then extends an arm in front of his head to maintain a stable position. He has pulled his legs in slightly to keep from nosing over into a dive, but not enough to impair the deployment of his back pack. Both arms are then extended forward as the ripcord releases the pack and the pilot chute springs free. Holding the basic stable spread position, the jumper allows the sleeve time to be extended by the two pilot chutes. In the last photograph the risers have been extended from the pack and the lines are being played out of the sleeve. When the last stow of lines comes free, the sleeve will slide free and air will inflate the canopy. (*Ralph White*)

A fast right turn is being initiated by this jumper. By drawing up into a tighter position, turns can be made faster. (*Joe Gonzales, U.S. Army*)

increase the force, the right hand may be pushed down while the left hand remains in the shoulder-high position. To stop the turn and reverse directions, the hands are rolled over to the other side so the left hand is low with the heel down and the heel of the right hand is now up. This is essentially the same principle as a propeller's twist.

Foot turns and leg turns are accomplished by raising and lowering the feet and legs. The body will swing toward the lower foot and away from the higher foot. To turn to the left, for example, the legs must swing to the right, so the right leg and foot are simply lowered while leaving the left leg and foot high. The positions are reversed to stop the turn and initiate a turn in the opposite direction.

Body turns are nearly always combined with arms and hands. The body is simply twisted to the right or left so the shoulder toward the turn is slightly lower than the other—again this is like the twist of a propeller.

THE BACKLOOP

The backloop is one of the simplest aerial maneuvers to accomplish and, no matter how sloppy the attempt, a loop (actually a backward somersault or back-flip) is nearly sure to result. However, a clean execution of any maneuver is necessary in style competition from both the standpoint of proper performance in the eyes of the judges and the time element. Lost seconds are lost points in competition and flailing around in the sky in an attempt to "swim" through a given maneuver takes too much time. No judge will award the full number of points for sloppy maneuvers no matter how fast they are performed so the loop must be both fast and clean.

To accomplish a loop or any other maneuver properly, the jumper must establish himself in relation to the ground and the horizon. First, he selects a reference point on the ground (a runway, highway, or fencerow). Second, he makes sure that he is starting from a flat stable position with the horizon comfortably visible in front, rather than too high or too low. With these two references determined before the start of maneuvers, precision turns, loops, and rolls can be accomplished with the maneuver always ending exactly where it began.

There is a tendency to roll off on one side during the backloop, but an understanding of the aerodynamics involved can correct the problem. Keeping the arms and legs spread gives a maximum of control over the rolling. However, putting the arms or legs close together is sometimes necessary to accomplish a clean maneuver. Each person must therefore adjust according to his need . . . spreading sometimes to gain stability and control, closing at other times to gain speed. In the illustrations you will seldom see a true textbook example of how any given maneuver is accomplished, because each individual alters the basic positions to suit his personal needs. It is sometimes necessary to alter a position and even completely violate a standard or accepted method in order to achieve the speed and attitude desired.

A backloop starts from the basic face-to-earth position. The arms are extended out and forward as the knees are drawn up to the body. This will swing the body up into an upright, seated position. The arms sweep down past the hips as if jumping rope, causing the body to fall over backward. The initial action of extending the arms and drawing up the knees will be enough to carry the body over the top of the loop into the inverted position. As the horizon comes back into view, the legs are extended and the arms moved back to the original stable spread

This sequence shows Rod Pack making a backloop. He might have gained more force by extending the arms farther in front at the beginning. (*Jim Lizzio*)

position to prevent a continuation of the loop beyond the original horizontal position. As the initial reference point on the ground comes back into view, the flared out, basic spread position is assumed.

Disorientation during early attempts is common and the novice may finish his loop as much as 90-degrees off his original heading. He may also find himself tilted over on one side and the horizon apparently standing vertical in front of him.

FRONTLOOP

The frontloop is usually done by accident a few times before the novice learns to maintain a stable position. Improper arch and looking down at the ground on exit during initial static-line student jumps often results in a forward loop. Later as the jumper begins free falls, he may execute a frontloop while pulling the ripcord, particularly with the two-hand method while looking at the ripcord. Again, it results from looking down and losing the arch. With this thought in mind, the skilled jumper can easily accomplish frontloops with precision. From a stable spread or relaxed frog position, the chin is tucked down, shoulders rolled forward, and legs extended. Arms are swept back to a delta position or even brought in to the sides as the body is bent sharply at the waist. The body immediately noses over and the legs are swung upward in a shuttlecock effect. This initiates a forward tumble or loop. Bending the legs and extending the arms slightly as the horizon appears again (upside down) will keep the body rotating while the hands and arms help prevent roll. As the body reaches the upright position and the horizon appears rightside up dead ahead, the arms are swung forward into a high spread to stop the rotation. The body then flares out into a stable spread position.

BARREL ROLL

Like the backloop, the barrel roll is a simple maneuver— except faster. Like a snaproll in an airplane, the reference point on the horizon is the secret. The jumper keeps his eyes glued to that reference point on the horizon the entire time so the body remains prone whether face-to-earth or back-to-earth or in between. A barrel roll is a fast maneuver that is little more

This jumper is about to perform a barrel roll—intentional or not. The right arm continues to hold air as the left arm is retracted. Once on his back he switches arms to continue the roll. (*Ralph White*)

than a swish of the right arm and a swish of the left. It is started from the basic spread position with the legs fully extended and only slightly separated. To roll clockwise, the left arm remains extended, but the right arm is pulled in to the chest. The body will instantly roll over in the back-to-earth position and momentum is maintained by extending the right arm as the left is withdrawn to the chest. The roll will continue back to the face-to-earth position and the left arm is quickly re-extended to prevent overshooting. Each arm is withdrawn for no more than a second before being re-extended.

BACK-TO-EARTH POSITION

The back-to-earth position is the most relaxed position a free-fall jumper can assume, but requires concentrated effort to avoid turns and uncontrolled spinning. A jumper who loses consciousness in free fall will always roll onto his back and begin turning. To roll onto the back, one arm is extended and the other withdrawn for a second—then re-extended immediately. Another method of turning onto the back is simply to bend forward slightly at the waist while maintaining the basic spread position. To get back in the face-to-earth position, arch the body and get the head back. Jumpers should make a conscious effort to experiment with back-to-earth delays periodically—they are unique, unpredictable, and exhilarating.

The back-to-earth position is one of the most difficult to maintain with stability, although the easiest to assume. With no reference points as in the face-to-earth position, the jumper may find himself pitching and yawing violently before beginning a slow rotation. Here Lt. Richard Economy demonstrates with full flight equipment the position being taught Air Force pilots in case of ejection at high altitude. (*Ralph White*)

The ability to initiate a given maneuver and then return to a stable fall is basic and essential to safety and enjoyment in the sport of parachuting. While there are some basic elementary maneuvers that are sure to be a part of any competition, maneuvers such as those just discussed, there is no limit to the combination of maneuvers the jumper can accomplish, if he thoroughly understands the aerodynamic forces that act upon his body. If he remembers that he is balanced on a huge ball of air, he can understand why certain things happen when he moves his body in certain ways. With this basic knowledge, he can invent maneuvers and experiment with positions to see what happens. These can be planned on the ground and then tried in the air, but like an airplane, the human body requires ample altitude for experimentation to allow suitable time to recover stability above the minimum opening altitude.

Those of us who began experimenting with maneuvers in free fall before established positions were discovered had great fun plunging out and assuming certain positions just to see what happened. Completely uncontrolled fall is exciting when recovery to stable fall is always within immediate reach, but uncontrolled fall is sheer terror when recovery is not within the jumper's grasp. Clawing a ripcord from its pocket while in chaotic tumbles and spins, I've seen that glob of unsheathed canopy shoot past my legs, trailed by a writhing mass of tan-

This jumper is obviously in fo some wild tumbling as he throw: himself all out of a symmetrica position. By assuming a basi spread, he will quickly recover t stable face-to-earth fall. (Ralp) White)

gled lines. In those split-second lifetimes I've heard myself screaming warnings from some detached point in time and space, and when, somehow all the lines clear themselves and the canopy blasts open, the shock jolts me back to reality. I am no longer viewing experience from some remote vantage point, but am a flesh-and-blood participant. Often a tiny trickle of blood verifies this truth, where a buckle digs into a shoulder or a connector link grazes the ear.

Early experiments with uncontrolled free fall and the recovery to stability were done without the benefit of padded harnesses or deployment devices. This meant that the position assumed at the time the ripcord was pulled was likely to be the position held at moment of opening shock. All of us had heard the gory stories of those head-down openings in which the victims dived out of their harnesses. Yet, there are few old-timers who hadn't had their helmets ripped from their head in a head-down opening—frequently giving up a small portion of skin with the helmet.

Today, with modern sport equipment, experimentation can still be as thrilling without being quite so punishing. The final test of skill for the jumper who thinks he can contend with any situation is that one hilarious fling into space without any attempt to stabilize. Somersault, spin, and flip-flop around the sky for a few thousand feet until the only reference point is your own body and your instruments (*never* lose track of time or altitude!), then flare out into a stable spread and enjoy the feeling of power that comes with gaining perfect control from total chaos. This stage is reached only after thorough mastery of body control and the ability to quickly and accurately read the instruments during total disorientation.

INSTRUMENTS

After acquiring a degree of confidence in himself and his equipment, making a dozen or more jumps, the sport parachutist can begin using instruments. These usually consist of a stopwatch and an altimeter, although many jumpers use only the altimeter.

The altimeter may be one especially designed and manufactured for sport parachuting or it may be a standard (sensitive) aircraft altimeter. Because of the rough treatment during routine parachuting operations, a jumper should make a habit of checking the accuracy of his instruments often, and he should never make the mistake of relying solely on instruments during long delays. The stopwatch can be easily checked against a fellow jumper's watch. The altimeter can be checked against the aircraft altimeter during the ascent to jump altitude and should be checked *again* at the time of exit to be sure the instrument is reading approximately the same as the aircraft. Both should be set at zero on the ground so the reading is the true altitude above the field and not elevation above sea level.

During the actual free fall, the jumper must not keep his eyes glued to the instruments, but read them periodically while also scanning the horizon (to maintain stable orientation) and watching for fellow jumpers in the sky.

A typical instrument panel as viewed by the jumper wearing it. Altimeter is at left and is always set at zero on the drop zone before takeoff. A stopwatch at the right starts and stops by pushing the button at top. Large sweep hand covers a 60-second face. Corners of the instrument board are rounded. (*Capital Parachuting Enterprises*)

Instruments are essential for a safe, delayed free fall. This altimeter is set to read altitude above the ground and is wrist-mounted. Instruments are usually mounted on the reserve chute, but the piggyback reserve rigs made wrist-mounts essential—for obvious reasons. This one reads to 12,000 feet with the last 2,500 feet marked in red. (*Steve Snyder Enterprises*)

Instruments can be wrong, so the parachutist does not rely entirely on them. He looks at the drop zone below, the target area, and other references. If he discovers that everybody else has pulled, chances are that he should too.

Obviously a thorough knowledge of the table of rate of descent in free fall is necessary before engaging in free-fall jumping. Prior to take-off, the jumper should decide how many seconds delay he plans to make. For example, if he is going to make a 30-second delay, he knows from the free-fall table that he will fall approximately 4,600 feet. In order to open at a safe 2,500 feet above the ground, he must jump from at least 7,100 feet. When he exits the jump plane, he starts his stopwatch. As he free falls he can see the altimeter unwinding and the stopwatch clicking off the seconds. As he nears his opening altitude the stopwatch should be ticking toward the thirtieth second and the altimeter should be nearing the 2,500 foot reading. If the stopwatch shows 30 seconds, but the altimeter reads only 4,000 feet, pull! Or if the altimeter shows 2,500 feet while the stop-watch reads only 20 seconds, pull! The jumper can check *later* to see which instrument was incorrect.

RATE OF DESCENT

Remember there is more to free falling than just falling. The uninformed may observe of sport parachutists that any nut can fling himself from a plane and drop like a rock. This premise is not totally inaccurate, although even dropping like a rock requires stability, and stability requires locking into a basic stable spread position for most jumpers (exceptions later). As discussed earlier, this position is assumed by extending the arms out from the shoulders with the legs extended and slightly spread. This cross-like position can be altered slightly provided there is always a balance of aerodynamic forces. For example, if the left leg is higher than the right leg, there are forces that will begin pushing the body to the left. But, if at the same time, the left arm is higher than the right arm, forces will be pushing the body to the right. Although this is a cockeyed position and awkward, the forces are balanced, and stable fall will result.

Most of us have encountered difficulty with goggles during free fall. If the hands are pulled up to the face to secure the goggles back in place, the result will be an immediate nose dive. The front half of the body has nothing to support it, while the back half has legs extended. The jumper becomes a human shuttlecock. This "Y" position results in higher rates of descent and may continue to accelerate to speeds of 160 to 200 mph instead of the so-called "terminal velocity" of the spread position of about 120 mph. An Italian named Canarrozzo popularized this position by folding the arms across the chest. It is possible to reach up with both hands and adjust your goggles without going into a Canarrozzo nose-dive. Bend the legs back at the knees to reduce drag at the rear while extending the elbows to increase drag up front. The resultant balance of forces allows the jumper to assume a relatively stable position. Because the body is drawn up into a tighter position, the area of drag is reduced and the rate of fall will increase slightly. This position may be referred to as the "frog" or "French frog" position. It allows the free-falling jumper to remain prone and horizontal

Rates of descent change with temperature, air density, atmospheric pressure, size and weight of the jumper, and even the type of jumpsuit worn, but the major factor is body position. The more area a jumper can cover, the slower he falls; the less area, the faster he falls. The jumpers pictured here are falling at different rates of descent. The bottom jumper has spread into a basic position to fall "slow," while the jumper above him is sweeping his arms back in an attempt to dive down to a lower level. He will glide away and miss his partner by a wide margin, however. He would do much better to draw up into a tighter position to increase his fall without tracking away in the process. It is not advisable to remain over a fellow jumper long since he may pull his ripcord and cause a midair collision. (*Ralph White*)

to the surface, yet fall faster than in the full spread position. His rate of fall can be adjusted by adjusting the amount of area his body covers.

Rate of fall can also be adjusted by the type of clothing worn. Large, baggy coveralls or jumpsuits slow the jumper's descent, while tight-fitting, tailored jumpsuits increase speed. A large person falls slightly faster than a small person, if both wear identical clothing and assume identical positions. Therefore, if a large and a small person are performing free-fall maneuvers in relation to each other ("relative work"), they will have to adjust positions to maintain identical rates-of-descent. The smaller, lighter person will have to draw up into a tighter position to fall slightly faster, while the larger person will flare out into a larger spread to fall slower. To make it easier, the larger person could wear a tailored nylon jumpsuit, while the smaller person wears a loose-fitting cotton jumpsuit; their difference in rate of fall would be considerably less than when they both wear identical clothing.

Departing from the stable spread or frog positions which allow the jumper to maintain a flat, horizontal position will result in a gliding effect. These positions allow the jumper to glide, or track, as much as a one-to-one ratio. The variations of the "delta" position determine the efficiency of the track. The legs remain extended and slightly spread, while the arms are swept back in varying degrees from the shoulder level. The hands always remain flat, fingers together (gloves help considerably), to act as ailerons and give control on the latitudinal axis. There is a tendency to roll as the arms are drawn down closer to the body and the rudder-like effect of the hands prevents this. A medium delta position is maintained by extending the arms at about forty-five degrees from the shoulder toward the waist. In this position, the body tends to tilt forward and slide or glide downhill. The rate of descent increases because the air is being deflected to the rear rather than being piled up beneath the body as in the stable fall. There is no aerodynamic lift created by this downhill glide, however, and this increased rate of forward speed is quickly neutralized by the increased rate of descent. Obviously, the longer time the body can glide, the farther it can go, but this time is reduced by the rapid descent. There is an optimum glide ratio that each jumper must determine for himself. This optimum glide cannot be appreciably increased.

It has been determined that a jumper may attain a horizontal speed of roughly 60 mph in the delta position. The danger involved in two jumpers approaching each other in opposite directions at up to 60 mph is obvious. Yet this is frequently the case when two inexperienced free-fallers attempt relative work, such as a baton pass, before they fully understand the forces involved. Unfortunately, midair collisions account for a significant number of injuries and fatalities in the sport. More experienced free-falling jumpers learn to approach at reduced speeds and then in such a way as to pass just to one side rather than head-on. Steve Snyder's automatic opener has saved a number of lives when the victim of "freight-training" regains consciousness under an inflated reserve chute. Unfortunately also, too many have been knocked unconscious who did not have an automatic opener. Other automatic openers are also available for sport which deploy the main parachute.

For maximum tracking the delta position is modified into the "max-track" position. In the maximum-track position, the body is humped in such a way that the larger, thicker portion of the head and shoulders create an airfoil and actually give a certain amount of lift. The head is drawn back and the shoulders are rolled forward, legs remain extended and arms are bent slightly and drawn in near the sides. Hands are cupped slightly and held near the hips. The body should be maintained in a head-down attitude at about thirty degrees below the horizontal. This position will vary from one individual to another, and each must determine his own optimum max-track position through experimentation. The rate of descent is greater than in a basic spread position and even as great as in a medium delta. The difference is in the significantly greater horizontal movement.

The ability to track, or move horizontally, during the descent before the chute is opened is helpful in correcting errors in spotting. When several persons are exiting the aircraft on the same pass over the target area, the person who spots and determines the exit point may make an error. Even assuming he is correct, the first person to leave and the last person to leave are separated horizontally by the speed of the aircraft during that span of time. Obviously both jumpers cannot be exactly in the right place in space. The first jumper may hold a stable spread position, while it is necessary for the last person to turn around and track back several hundred yards to get back to the proper point in space where he can reach the target after opening.

The ability to track can also prevent some embarrassing situations. A former jump student of mine and I were making a fun jump for accuracy only, but from 7,500 feet with a thirty-second delay. He and I had been jumping at different clubs and had not jumped together for more than a year. During this time, he had purchased the recently developed Para-Commander chute and was becoming fairly accurate. I was wearing my favorite old rag—a 7-TU modification with nearly 300 jumps on it. He insisted that since I had such an old chute and could

This jumper has just exited the aircraft and has already drawn his hands back to his sides to decrease wind resistance. He will nose over like a bomb and gain speed. This is done when competing in style events because the faster the speed, the quicker the series can be executed. It may also be used by jumpers who are doing relative work such as building a star—again, to get down fast and catch up with the rest of the jumpers who may have exited several seconds ahead. By arching his back and cupping his hands perpendicularly to his thighs, he assumes an excellent tracking position. (*Joe Gonzales, U.S. Army*)

not maneuver as well as he, that I spot for us. He insisted that I spot for myself to be in the best possible place and he would exit immediately behind me. Even though he might be a little farther out than I, he could easily bomb the target in his P-C, he explained. I smiled and thanked him for his kindness to old has-beens like myself and agreed to do the spotting. As we made our final jump run toward the target, I got out early and signaled the student to get ready. He crowded up to the door as I positioned on the wheel outside. I nodded for him to follow and pushed away nearly a mile short of the target—then humped into a max-track and hoped he wasn't watching me. He wasn't. I landed respectably in the sawdust area and had finished a coke back at the hangar when he arrived on horseback from an adjoining farm.

More than one visitor has been initiated into a new club by having the group take him far off the spot and then all track back to the right point, leaving him a mile or two off in the wrong direction.

To correct a bad spot—whether it was intentional or unintentional—is not too difficult. When jumping with jokesters or others whom you suspect might be leading you astray, it is a good idea to keep an eye on them as you follow them out of the plane. If you see the other jumpers humping their shoulders and assuming a max-track, it's a good idea to swing around and follow them. If you find you cannot reach the proper opening point even by tracking, you have an alternate method of reaching the target. If you are upwind of the target, simply open high (but be sure the sky above you is clear if others are jumping with you). By opening high, you remain in the air longer and drift with the wind longer. The farther out you are, the higher you must open, if you are to remain aloft long enough to reach the target area. Conversely, if you find you are downwind of the target or nearly over it, a low opening (but no lower than safety rules permit) will allow you to reach the ground sooner and prevent drifting farther than is absolutely necessary.

JUMPING WITH OTHERS

When jumping alone, or with only one or two others whom you can keep in constant view during free fall, a high opening creates no hazard. However, under no circumstances is the canopy deployed above the jointly agreed-upon opening altitude when a group of jumpers are falling together. Even when the agreed opening point is reached, it is a good idea for the parachutist to give the "wave-off" signal to any possible jumpers directly over him. The wave-off is given by sweeping the hands from the outstretched basic spread position in to the head and back, bending the arms at the elbows.

The smart jumper avoids being near other jumpers below 4,000 feet. If he finds himself immediately over another jumper at 3,000 feet, he should make every effort to get away and be especially alert for the jumper below to pull. If this occurs, the pilot chute can be batted aside. In the days of unsleeved can-

Relative work is the ultimate in sport jumping. Only someone who has experienced it can understand the pure pleasure of drifting across the sky to meet a friend some 10,000 feet above the ground. Note the glide path of each jumper is just to the right of the other to avoid a head-on collision in the event their closing speed is too great. (*Ralph White*)

opies, it would be almost impossible to avoid entanglement. However, because of the sleeve-deployment or bag-deployment, the opening is slowed, and the upper jumper can escape by keeping alert. An alternate choice when directly over another jumper as the opening altitude is approached is to give a wave-off signal and pull slightly higher. These are situations that

A major cause of parachuting fatalities is the midair collision of jumpers with jumpers or of jumpers with canopies. When striking a canopy, the upper jumper usually suffers severe lacerations while the lower jumper is knocked unconscious after having his canopy destroyed. Carl Boenish was filming Ken Vos (left) and Willie Manbo (right) at close range and then began drifting back for a long-range view as Vic Weatherford opened below. (The lower jumper always has the "right of way.") Boenish just missed hitting the canopy himself as his camera recorded this jumper's nightmare. Vos and Manbo snapped 13 suspension lines—each line having a tensile strength of 550 pounds. Vos was hospitalized for several days with a broken jaw, cracked ribs, and severe facial lacerations that required plastic surgery. Manbo was hospitalized with a fractured shoulder. Weatherford's canopy was destroyed, but he landed safely on his reserve chute. All three recovered to jump again. Carl Boenish filmed *The Gypsy Moths* which starred Burt Lancaster and is recognized as one of the best free-fall cameramen in the sport. (*Carl Boenish*)

will not occur among skilled free-fall jumpers who avoid ever getting into such a predicament. Before boarding the aircraft, all jumpers should agree on the opening altitude when planning the jump.

RELATIVE WORK

After a jumper is proficient in his aerial maneuvers (that is, he can adjust his rate of descent in free fall and move horizontally) he is sure to engage in relative work. This is jumping in relation to one or more other jumpers to accomplish such basic things as passing an object, taking photographs, etc. Most parachutists agree that this is the real fun of the sport—when that sense of weightlessness is most apparent. To see another human being drift serenely across in front of you, gently rising and falling as he approaches, is an experience second to none.

When two jumpers are planning to pass a baton, they should carefully plan the jump on the ground, walking through movements to see exactly how they will hold the baton during the pass, when one will release it to the other, what the second will do with it when he has to pull his ripcord, where he will put

A baton marks a milestone in every jumper's life. Here Chuck Seymour cautiously closes in on the baton. To reach out for the baton would be a mistake and cause him to drift backward. Here he unconsciously executes a left turn using only his legs. He is not wearing goggles. The 120 mph wind distorts his facial features. (*U.S. Navy*)

it after the chute is opened and his hands must be free. It is best for the *first* jumper to carry the baton and maintain a relatively stable position until the second jumper has come down to his level and begun moving in. Should one drop below, it is necessary for the upper jumper to ease himself down on the level with the first again, always moving toward each other slowly but deliberately. Cupping the hands in the frog position and gently straightening the legs slightly from the frog position will gently nudge the chutist forward. A common error in early baton pass attempts is the tendency to become over-anxious and reach out for the baton, or for the person with the baton to extend it out to the approaching partner. A modified frog position must be used to avoid the buffeting, pitching and yawing that result from a high, stable spread. If the legs remain bent as they are in the frog position, but the arms are extended to hand off or to accept the baton, the result is obvious—the body will rise slightly in front, lower in the rear, and a backward glide will occur. The two jumpers then drift backward away from each other and the more they stretch to make contact, the more intense becomes the drift apart. Therefore, they must keep the hands near the normal frog position and approach right up to final contact in that position. After a few contacts are made and each jumper becomes familiar with his partner's flight characteristics as well as his own, quick and confident contacts can be made within a few seconds.

An ample amount of time is required for early attempts and, in sport parachuting, time is altitude. Never become so involved in relative work that awareness of altitude and time is lost. If the contact is not made by 4,000 feet, the wave-off should be given and the jumpers should get clear of each other for the remaining 1,500 feet or so before opening. This is a good safety margin. It should not be shortened even though there is an almost irrepressible urge to continue when contact is only inches away. Sometimes those last few inches can take too long. A second attempt may never be possible, if this one is pursued beyond the realm of safety.

To many sport parachutists the art of free falling is the major enjoyment. I share this opinion and compare it to a person who enjoys diving more than swimming. A person who cannot

Relative work should be accomplished with ease and grace, each participant moving slowly and deliberately until gentle contact is made. Obviously artist-jumper Frederick Ely has experienced relative work with a jumper who was less than skilled in the art of passing a baton. A real danger exists when jumpers get over-anxious and track head-on toward each other at up to 60 mph. (Sky Diver Magazine)

swim finds it extremely difficult to become proficient as a diver, since swimming out after each dive is necessary to complete the cycle. The same analogy can apply to sport parachutists who enjoy the delayed free falls, but not particularly the parachute descent and landing. A significant number of jumpers consider the jump over when the ripcord is pulled. The real thrill and pleasure come with the weightlessness and aerial maneuvering during free fall. Opening the parachute is only a necessary step in the cycle like swimming out of the pool after the dive.

The newer, exotic parachute designs that allow greater comfort and greater control may make the descent and landing more fun for the present generation of jumpers, but to many of the old-timers who have descended in non-steerable canopies into thorn trees, rock quarries, rivers, and power lines, there is a certain amount of fatherly tolerance for those who will never know what they missed. Like war experiences, they are nice to reminisce about, but hell to live through.

To clear up any misunderstandings about who are the old-timers, they are those who jumped in pre-Para-Commander days. Many of the most famous have been defrocked now by a generation that isn't satisfied with jump stories or impressed with past performances. Like some of our heroes of American history who have been reduced to mere mortals with human weaknesses, some of our heroes of sport parachuting in America have even been accused and abused.

The entire sport probably owes more to Jacques Istel and Lew Sanborn than to any other men in the history of our sport, but when they made it a profession and dared charge a fee for qualified instruction and quality equipment, they were subjected to abuse. For years there was a feeling that boarded on the divine, relative to parachuting. Those few who were recognized as authorities and experts in the sport held godlike power over the masses, even though they did not necessarily seek that power. Those days and those men are gone now—in only a *decade*. Today, there are hundreds of excellent sport parachute clubs with skilled and competent jumpers anxious to instruct and assist the novice. Equipment is available at reasonable costs from many sources. Anyone who wants to learn the sport or even make "just one jump to see what it's like" will have no trouble in locating competent instructors and quality equipment. Parachuting has become a full-fledged, respectable, recognized sport.

7

POUR LE SPORT
Competition and Sport Jumping

When the sport jumper has achieved the degree of competency that he can control both his emotions (the ability to think clearly under extremely foreign situations) and his body (respond quickly and accurately), he is ready to take command of his equipment. He should have determined his own ability and limitations during his training and early free-fall experience. Now he will learn the limitations of his equipment.

Before moving on to advanced techniques of the sport, he must learn to trust his instruments, but still be aware that malfunctions in a stopwatch or altimeter are possible. He must trust his parachutes (both of them) with his very life, but still know they can malfunction and that corrective measures must be taken quickly if they do.

Certainly a jumper would be unable to exit the plane, if he dwelt on the many possibilities of "What if . . . ?" But thorough knowledge is the source of strength. The knowledge that he has both the capability and the emotional stability to quickly and correctly take necessary action in the event of an emergency carries over into his everyday situations. If ever there were a sport that requires self-confidence and independence, parachuting is that sport. When he finds himself splitting the atmosphere at 174 feet per second somewhere between eternity above and eternity below, he will never be more alone or less able to get a helping hand. Although parachuting for sport is anything but a lonely sport, it affords a certain amount of solitude second to no other sport. His only companion is his parachute and an affection for that first parachute is as real as any other first love.

A few years ago sport jumping consisted of two categories: *style*—the ability to perform a series of given maneuvers in the shortest possible time; and *accuracy*—the ability to manipulate the parachute canopy in such a way as to land on or close to a specified target. These are still the basic features of most competition jumping and a significant portion of "fun jumping" involves one or both of these skills.

In recent years, however, the competition, like the parachutes, has divided and subdivided into an almost endless array of more challenging events. Some competitions include groups of jumpers who must act as a team *in the air,* almost like a basketball team might on the court. Competition may center around the formation of "stars," a sort of ring-around-a-rosy in the sky. Any number of jumpers from three-up may exit and join up to form a star; each point being a jumper. For example, eight persons who join together form an eight-man star. The star is formed one person at a time. No fair all joining hands and then exiting en masse!

Another team event may require a baton pass by two or more jumpers. The first recorded baton pass in the United States was made in 1958 by Steve Snyder and Chuck Hilliard, two aeronautical engineering students at Georgia Tech. Both went on to become leaders in the world of aviation. Steve has invented and manufactured many safety devices for the sport, while Chuck took to flying aerobatics in national and world championship style.

As new accomplishments are made in parachuting activities —the "star" or the baton pass—they frequently become a part of special events in competitions. These are for those who want

The cheapo (military surplus canopy with modification) at left and the lopo (low porosity sport parachute) at right were all there were in the early 1960's and they did a good job, but they are no match for the later, more sophisticated designs. (*Joe Gonzales, U.S. Army*)

The Para-Commander revolutionized sport parachuting and made the competition jumper an ace. (*Air Force Academy*)

a greater challenge than style and accuracy and often the jumper who fails at the basic events may find himself with a trophy or a cash prize in one of the specialty contests.

One old favorite specialty event that is rapidly dying is the hit-and-run event. A bell or buzzer is located at the center of the target. A jumper is timed from the moment of touchdown until he rings the bell. If he lands closely enough, he may strike the bell with his foot or hand at the time of touchdown, or if he lands a few yards away, he may be fleet of foot enough to ring the bell sooner than a person who landed closer. Even here, the old pros are easy to tell from the amateurs. Those in the know realize it's better to hit a few yards upwind and be pulled toward the target than to land inches short on the downwind side and be dragged away before hitting the buzzer. These are events that are in the novelty class, designed to give the spectators a show and allow the less experienced jumpers a chance to compete. With the present day sport canopies making dead-center landings possible, nine out of ten jumps, the hit-and-run event would be all hit and no run.

In serious—almost deadly—competition on an international or national scale, championships at this writing are still primarily determined by accuracy and style. These are the two events which will be discussed.

STYLE

Style jumping is the art of controlled free fall. Until recently, the type of parachute worn was of no consequence, since the jumper was judged only on how he performed during free fall and not on where he landed after his parachute was opened. This has changed as equipment affects free-fall characteristics. In the early 1960's, style quickly became a matter of speed. The international series became the basic maneuver. This amounted to a figure eight with a backloop followed by another figure eight and a backloop. A figure eight is a 360-degree turn followed by an immediate 360-degree turn in the opposite direction. The direction of the opening turn and succeeding turns might have been predetermined by drawing lots before takeoff or by ground signals given to the competitor after he was out of the plane and falling stable on a given heading.

For example, the competitor might be given a ground signal

that indicated he was to start his first figure eight with a left turn, then his second figure eight with a right turn. He would then proceed to accomplish this as follows: fall stable on heading until signal is given and understood—up to 10 seconds was usually allowed before the competitor was required to begin his maneuver. The instant he swung left off his original required heading, the judges began timing him and reading his maneuvers through ground optical instruments. The competitor proceeded with a left turn 360 degrees until he reached his original heading, then immediately reversed direction and made a 360-degree right turn until he was back on the original heading; now a quick backloop and back on heading; now a right turn of 360 degrees to original heading; a quick reverse left turn 360 degrees to original heading; and a final backloop still on original heading. Flare-out position was assumed and the judges stopped the watches. To achieve an advanced parachutist (C) license in the United States, the applicant has to accomplish this series of maneuvers in eighteen seconds or less. The expert license (D) requires considerably more skill (see appendix for license requirements).

Even with cumbersome parachutes and uniforms of a decade ago, the international series could be done in about twelve seconds by most competent, experienced jumpers. Since all competent jumpers could accomplish these maneuvers accurately, speed became the important element. Sometimes the time was given in which to compete the series of maneuvers and bonus points could be earned by performing them accurately in less time than was allotted. The bonus points determined the highest score—the winner.

Also in the early 1960's, style jumpers realized that something would have to be done to offer less restrictions by equipment, if they were to increase their speed and reduce style times. It was thought that removing the reserve might offer less restrictions, but this would be unsafe. So the reserve was redesigned slightly to fit the contour of the body—a sort of wrap-around reverse in front. Within a few years jumpers found that tucking the body greatly increased speed in turns, but again, even with tied-down, contoured reserves, there was restricted movement. Even so, times were getting down to the ten-second range.

Security Parachute Company designed their piggyback pack which moved the reserve around to the back, riding in a separate compartment above the main canopy and leaving the front of the jumper as slick as a button. Altimeters were redesigned by Steve Snyder into a thin disc that could be mounted on the wrist like a watch, since an altimeter mounted on a reserve now would require an extra eyeball in the back of the head. The reserve on the new Security piggyback rig was activated by pulling a lollipop type ripcord mounted on the opposite side of the harness from the main ripcord. With this new streamlined harness and Pioneer's new Para-Commander sport canopy, the U.S. Parachute Team headed for the Seventh World Parachuting Championships in Leutkirch, West Germany. The event took place in August, 1964. Despite the streamlined equipment, the U.S. team failed to take the style event and, for the second time in a row, Russian Evgenij Tkachenko became the world style champion with an average time of 8.5 seconds and wearing a reserve chute on his stomach. The reserve on the front obviously did not present the problem originally thought and the piggyback rig had no appreciable effect on style times.

Style judges station themselves and their optical instruments at different positions in order to view a jumper from a number of different angles. The judge reads his score to a scorekeeper. Judging style remains a sore point in international competition and politics sometimes influence a judge's evaluation. Video-tapes may soon be required for style judging. Here USPA judge Ron Radhoff focuses on a contestant.

When Security Parachute Company released the piggyback harness, it was a major innovation and offered many advantages. This jumper has a stopwatch mounted on his left wrist to check himself on a style jump. Later style jumpers moved the reserve chute back to the front, however, to keep the center of gravity lower and allow a tighter position. (*Ralph White*)

While waiting their turns, fellow competitors may check the style performance of a jumper even though official judges are scoring the event. Doug Metcalfe (at optical instrument), 1970 U.S. Style Champion, checks times with fellow jumpers as a style competitor drifts into the packing area behind.

Within a few years style jumpers found the answer with a much shorter backpack and a higher-riding reserve on the chest. Ted Strong's Stylemaster rig and North American Aerodynamics' Mini System jump set were especially designed to meet the needs of the serious style competitor.

Style requires smooth transition from one maneuver to another. The second turn of the first figure eight should lead directly into the backloop and the backloop lead smoothly into the first turn of the second figure eight. Do not confuse smooth with sloppy (which results in the loss of points). Being extremely fast is of no benefit, if all points are lost through sloppy maneuvers.

The style event at the Seventh World Championships was as follows: The jumper was awarded 200 points entering the aircraft. He jumped from 2,000 meters (6,600 feet) and was graded during free fall on style and aerial maneuvers. No landing accuracy points were awarded. The contestant departed the aircraft on a fixed ground signal. After the jumper left the plane, a visual ground signal was displayed for five seconds which indicated one of three predetermined series of maneuvers the jumper was to execute. The contestant was then required to execute the proper maneuver sequence of 360-degree turns and backloops as fast and smoothly as possible within twenty seconds. Five bonus points were awarded for each second under twenty. He lost ten points for each second late after the twentieth second. Points also were deducted for failure to complete turns or loops, undershooting or overshooting turns or loops, loss of control, or exceeding seconds.

Because fast maneuvers require drawing the body up into a tight frog position, judging becomes increasingly difficult even for professionals using special optics. As early as summer of 1964, top professional judge (and editor of *Skydiver Magazine*) Lyle Cameron was pointing to the extreme difficulty judges were facing in timing and judging style accurately because, as competitors approached the limiting time, there was scarcely a second separating the fastest time from the slowest time. Style requires an all-out effort on the part of the judges as well as the contestants.

Manipulating the parachute canopy to land in a designated spot has been the goal of every parachutist. Until the Security Cross-Bow canopy and Pioneer's Para-Commander (both coming on the market in the summer of 1964) there were no truly steerable parachute canopies designed from the ground up with the thought of steerability. As far back as the 1930's, jumpers had been taking scissors to standard parachute canopies and modifying them into so-called "steerable" canopies.

The original Russian blank gore was probably the first that gave more than minimum control. The Derry slot canopy of the smokejumpers in the late 1930's and into even present-day smokejumper rigs allowed the parachutist to turn, but afforded very little forward motion. After the blank gore came numerous other modifications of standard parachute canopies. Eventually modifications reached their limit—probably the seven-gore TU modifications of the late 1950's and early 1960's. That is to say, there is only a certain amount of material which can be cut away from a standard 28-foot diameter parachute canopy before the rate of descent becomes intolerable. Although the TU canopy (its design is generally credited to Loy Brydon) was given credit for ten or twelve mph forward speed and fast-turning capabilities, it also dropped at better than 21 feet per second with an average-weight jumper in the harness.

In 1964, the Cross-Bow and the Para-Commander were both put on the market as the first truly steerable sport parachutes designed from the beginning as a sport parachute and not a modification of anything else; a brand new species developed to meet the demands of a sport which had outgrown the scissors-and-masking-tape era. Without getting involved in the merits or technical data of either canopy, it is safe to say that these two canopies put the fun back in sport jumping and eliminated many of the dangers. The primary danger in parachuting is not being killed when the canopy fails to inflate properly, but rather *where* the parachutist lands *after* his parachute is properly inflated. Trees, power lines, rivers, lakes, highways, buildings, ditches, and rocks are only a few of the objects which can cause serious, if not fatal injuries. More than ninety percent of the injuries sustained in the sport of jumping are from landing somewhere other than the target area prepared for landings. Roughly thirty-three percent of the fatalities over the past ten years were due to drowning!

With the newer, fully steerable parachutes available, accuracy became a matter of centimeters instead of yards. Within months after the Para-Commander and Cross-Bow were on the open market, jumpers were scoring dead-center landings frequently enough to make at least a couple of dead-centers necessary in order to win the event. Judging became more critical. Since the dead-center disc is smaller than the jumper's boot, the heel or toe had to be carefully placed for a true dead-center landing to be scored. Those of us who remember when we considered ourselves lucky to land on the airport property found these new sport parachutes took some of the thrill out of parachuting, but put the sport into a category of skill more than luck. Those of us who did not switch to the newer sport chutes found the old modified canopies of little competitive value.

One of the first major money events, held at Stone Mountain, Georgia, drew top contestants from all across the United States, including several national champions. Nearly all used PC or XBO canopies, including money-winner Bob Holler. My good friend Bob Vaughan entered the events with the older TU modified canopies. Afterwards, he compared himself to Roscoe Turner at a jet pilot's convention.

Accuracy in landing requires a great deal of skill and just a dab of luck. Normally in average, weekend-type fun jumping, the jumper turns into the wind and makes his landing facing into the wind. The forward speed of the parachute is reduced by the speed of the wind, so the landing speed is minimized. However, slight variations in wind, updrafts from uneven heading on the surface, and even movements of the steering toggles that trap or spill air, will greatly affect the accuracy of landing when the approach is slow and gentle. These same conditions apply to an airplane landing at very slow speed for a gentle three-point touchdown. Accuracy is difficult.

In competition accuracy jumps, with all but the high performance wing canopies, the landing is made downwind. Again using an airplane as a comparison, this might be compared to the power-on, wheel landing where maximum control is maintained right up to touch-down. By approaching the target from the upwind position, the jumper can crisscross the downwind drift then, at the moment that he is in the exact position, he swings his parachute into a direct line and drives straight into the target. The approach is comparatively fast and rough. He must manipulate the steering toggles with the delicate touch of an artist, taking care to avoid abrupt or violent changes in the steering. A sudden attempt to correct by pulling hard on a steering toggle will change the flight characteristics of the canopy and swing the jumper like a pendulum. The pendulum movement usually causes greater inaccuracy than would result from a light touch and gentle movement.

Because the downwind landing is usually rough, the target area in any competition is cushioned with pea gravel, woodchips or other impact-absorbing material. This area usually extends at least twenty feet or more from the center of the target so the jumper can stay in the padded area even if he does not hit dead-center. If the contestant is landing more than twenty feet from dead-center, he may as well turn upwind and land gently because his score will not be good enough to put him in the competition. Judges in most contests will not even measure the distance if it exceeds five meters.

Until the winged designs hit the market in mid-1970, all canopies—from the Para-Commander to the cheapo—would be driven downwind into the target. With a winged canopy that may have a forward speed of 30 mph, landing downwind would not only be inaccurate, it would be unhealthy. Although these canopies can be slowed to only three or four mph, an upwind landing into a brisk breeze can be accurate.

If the jumper can maneuver his canopy in such a way that he is within a body's length of the target, he may swing his body in the harness and land flat on his back in an attempt to get his heel nearer the center disc. Care must be taken that the heel strikes first, of course, as the measurement will be made from the first point of body contact.

When the reserve chute is mounted on the front of the harness, it should be unsnapped on one side so it hangs out of the contestant's line of sight to the target. It is difficult to strike a tiny disc with the toe when the vision is blocked. Normally the ripcord handle on a reserve is on the right side of the reserve and it is this side which should remain hooked so the handle is up. If the right side is unhooked so the reserve hangs on the left with the handle down it may be jarred loose, releasing the reserve canopy.

Some contestants may also release the chest strap while approaching the target to allow the shoulder straps and risers to spread, in hopes of a slower descent on the downwind approach. The value of this practice is questionable, but the danger of falling out of the harness is real and obvious. I find it hard to decide which would be worse—falling completely out of the harness some hundred feet above the ground or making a downwind landing in pea gravel while suspended upside down by the leg straps.

Accuracy judges Art Armstrong (left) and Phil Miller (right) keep a close eye on contestant Billy Lockward as he hits the pea gravel 60 centimeters short of the target disc. He still scored second place overall to collect $1,000 second prize money at this Las Vegas meet. Lockward helped his U.S. team win the World Parachuting Championship in 1968 when, on his 2,000th jump, he cranked out a 7.6-second series and then scored a dead-center landing.

Security's Cross-Bow parachute was a marked improvement over anything on the market at the time, but soon fell from favor as the Para-Commander came into regular use. (*Jim Pol*)

Accuracy events nowadays are measured in centimeters rather than yards. Here Bobby Letbetter scores a dead-center landing. He was awarded the Distinguished Flying Cross, had participated in 73 World Parachuting Records and had more than 1,450 jumps to his credit when he was killed in a North Vietnamese ambush. (*Joe Gonzales, U.S. Army*)

Team accuracy requires special skill to attain this perfect team stack as demonstrated by members of the Air Force Academy. (*Air Force Academy*)

A competitor starts his stopwatch as he exits over the target area below. (*Ralph White*)

"If it's not too windy, how come that judge just blew away?" says Pete Negrette as Lyle Cameron demonstrates a backloop in the pea gravel. Judge Art Armstrong is at far right. (*Ralph White*)

Space prevents detailed instructions in the approach and landing in accuracy jumping, but there are some basic concepts that can be applied. With these fundamentals, practice can bring desired results. If there were no wind blowing, the target would be the point of a large, imaginary cone. The diameter of this cone grows larger with altitude. Once the parachute canopy is inflated, the jumper should maneuver into this imaginary cone and remain within it right down to contact with the target. As the altitude decreases, the diameter of the cone decreases and the amount of movement across the cone decreases. If the wind is blowing, the cone must be tilted upwind. The jumper must maneuver his canopy back and forth across this ever-narrowing area until he knows he is ready to drive straight toward the target. If he makes his final turn too soon, he will not descend fast enough and will over-shoot the target. If he waits too late to make his break for the target, he will fall short. So it becomes a matter of judging the distance out, the height above the ground, the angle of approach, the wind, the capabilities of the parachute, and the delicacy with which the jumper manipulates his controls.

Most modern parachutes have "brakes" that can slow the forward speed. It is recommended that the final approach to the target be made with some brakes applied. As the target comes closer, more or less pressure can be applied to adjust the closing speed, but it must be applied gently to avoid sudden surges of power followed by a backswing. Turns are to be avoided now and the approach should have been made in such a way that no further turns are made after the final break for the target.

When the approach is made properly, the final turn and run toward the target requires a minimum of manipulation of controls. The contestant who is frantically sawing up and down on his control lines and flailing in the harness just before impact is seldom a winner. While he may succeed once in a while, he will lose far more than he wins. Present-day scoring requires consistently good scores on a number of jumps in any given event.

SAFETY REGULATIONS

Because there are certain dangers involved in any active sport, rules of safety are set up within the ranks to govern the sport. Parachuting for sport owes its very survival to a number of persons who set up basic rules for self-regulation. Where dangerous parachuting was conducted throughout the country, states passed regulations forbidding parachute jumps. Every time a parachutist spattered the countryside, laws were passed to further restrict parachuting. There was no distinction made between safe jumping and dangerous jumping. From past experience, legislators decided all parachuting was unsafe, but through education of the public and the legislators, parachuting laws were repealed or changed to comply with those standards of safety and conduct set up by the parachutists themselves.

Until the 1960's, the Federal Aviation Administration did not recognize a parachutist as a human being. He was officially considered "an object" dropped from a plane, and the pilot was held responsible. Obviously pilots were not anxious to be held responsible, and they were understandably cautious about whom they flew. This accounts for the extremely high percentage of parachutists who are also pilots. Only a parachutist felt confident of another parachutist's ability, so they frequently flew each other. Now things have changed, and the FAA officially recognizes a parachutist as a person capable of controlling his descent in such a way that he can land without undue danger either to himself or to persons and property on the ground. The current FAA regulations reflect the influence of parachutists themselves and the official safety regulations of the national parachuting organization, the United States Parachute Association.

Safety rules and recommended procedures help prevent accidents. Although the man below always has the right of way, things get crowded near the target. Here Bill Dzoba, above, has his air captured by Danny Bates, parachute below, on approach to the target. Dzoba settled knee-deep, then ran across the canopy and jumped off. Both landed safely, in the pea gravel.

Recently added to major competitions is the relative work event. Here a team is building a star. (*Bob Buquor*)

As the number of parachutists increases each year, more restrictions are imposed. Since these rules are constantly changing, persons interested in current regulations should write USPA headquarters or the FAA in Washington, D.C., to secure the latest rulings. Any first-rate jump club in the country should have the latest information available and comply with those regulations in order to continue active participation in the sport.

NIGHT JUMPING

Jumping at night is currently permissible when done in accordance with FAA and USPA regulations. This is exhilarating and exciting for both the participants and the spectators on the ground. On my first night jump, I made a short ten-second delay. The pilot—who had never flown a night jump—reported to the observers on the ground that he never saw my chute open. This was understandable, because in ten seconds I had dropped more than 1,100 feet below the plane. Typical of those flat-circular, non-steerable canopy days, I landed in waist-deep water half a mile from the hangar's lights. While searchers probed the darkness with flashlights for my mangled body, my wife clung to the hope that somehow I had survived the plunge. When I finally wandered into the hangar after the jump, she was on the verge of hysteria. I explained to the pilot that in the future he need not expect to see the parachute open on night parachute jumps.

Looking down from several thousand feet over the country-side at night is a beautiful sight; the tiny lights below give a fairyland appearance to everything. But there are difficulties in night jumping. Getting an accurate wind drift reading is diffi-cult. Dropping a light that is known to have an accurate rate of descent is the best method, but it frequently becomes lost in the maze of lights scattered below. Most night jumpers rely on the average wind directions from the day and recognize that the wind usually dies considerably with darkness. With today's high-performance canopies wind is no problem on night jumps, if the proper spot for exit is determined. This, however, is a major problem.

Probably the best method of marking the target in such a way that it is easily spotted at night from several thousand feet up is to use a flare on the target. However, flares are hot and must be quickly removed as a jumper approaches to prevent burning either him, his canopy, or his equipment. The jumper must wear lights to make himself visible to other jumpers and to airplanes. He must have some means of lighting his instru-ments on long delays. On short delays of ten seconds or less, he can simply count. When a number of jumpers are in the air together, flashlights can be carried for searching each other out. Just don't drop it! There is a certain unique thrill that comes with drifting out into unknown and unlighted terrain at night. Not only is it impossible to know exactly when you will strike the ground, but often it is impossible to tell what you will land on

Not men from Mars—just two jumpers after a night drop. The rotating beacons strapped to the helmets are required by safety regulations to prevent midair collisions. (*Joe Gonzales, U.S. Army*)

or in—maybe ground, maybe water, maybe a tree, a stump, a fence or fencepost, or maybe a building. This is when that flashlight comes in handy . . . as well as when finding your way back to civilization.

FLARES AND SMOKE BOMBS

Night jumps are sometimes made with flares, day jumps often with smoke. Both provide better viewing by the spectators. Both can be dangerous and should be handled with care. There are a number of commercially produced flares and smoke bombs available to the sport parachutist and a large number are secured through military sources, often illegally. Although both can be hand-held if properly mounted for that purpose, some of the

Smoke can be hand-held or mounted on a boot-bracket as illustrated here. Ace free-fall photographer Chip Maury with an early wrist-mounted Nikon camera has the tables turned on him by fellow jumper-photographer Ed Kruse who took this shot. (*Ed Kruse, U.S. Navy*)

military smoke bombs get extremely hot, occasionally starting grass fires when dropped. Boot brackets for clamping smoke bombs or flares to the boot are also available and this is the recommended method of using them. A word of caution when using boot-mounted smoke bombs and flares: do not bend the legs back in a tight frog position or you may make *yourself* into a flare! Participating in a mass exhibition jump, Larry Estep did not realize he was about to set himself afire during his delayed free fall. On the ground he found that he had burned away a portion of his jumpsuit and badly scorched the saddle of his harness. The boot brackets have also been known to entangle with a deploying parachute during unstable openings. So the brackets can be as dangerous as the smoke bomb or flare when used by an unskilled jumper. Generally, the use of smoke and flares should be limited to advanced jumpers.

CLOUDS

Although parachuting through clouds has been outlawed by FAA regulations, there are many who feel this should not be illegal. Possibly because we had been dropping through clouds for years before somebody decided to make it illegal. The danger, of course, is in colliding with an airplane. However, when a medium-sized fluffy cumulus cloud is observed for several minutes and no planes are seen flying near it, there is little chance a plane has taken refuge and is hiding in there. Large cloud banks that cover a significant area of the sky are another story, but there is a special enjoyment that comes with picking out a lonely little cumulus cloud and then leaping into it like it's a big feather bed.

On one particular high jump with demonstration partner Jim Thompson, we exited at 18,000 feet above scattered clouds that were topping at about 6,000 feet. We found that our fall was carrying us into a rather large cloud, so we maintained stable fall to prevent collision. After we had fallen two miles toward the clouds, they suddenly took on the appearance of solid bodies. For a split second, I had the sensation of impacting a solid surface as Jim and I struck the cloud with a poof. The cloud was thin and light and we were quickly out again, but falling

Using hand-held smoke to keep him oriented, the author drops into a heavy cloud before regulations prohibited cloud-jumping.

through several thousand feet of cloud can result in total disorientation.

Another time I carried a hand-held smoke bomb into a cloud that extended from a base at 3,000 feet to a rolling dome at 10,000 feet and growing. Starting from 12,000 feet I entered the top of the cloud in about fifteen seconds and descended through a light gray mist. Holding a modified high stable spread position, I tried to keep track of my instruments, but water vapor condensed on both instruments and goggles, making reading difficult. As I wiped the goggles and instruments with a gloved hand, I could see that my smoke was no longer trailing up but was trailing back over my right shoulder. Then it was streaming directly sideways from my left hand across in front of my face and past my right hand. Although I had no sensation of falling, it was obvious I was falling on one side. From then on, I turned my body in relation to the streaming smoke and kept it flowing straight up from the bomb. Near the base of the cloud formation the light gray had turned to dark gray and finally to nearly complete darkness. I broke through the bottom of the cloud like dropping through a trap door. After I opened my parachute I realized that I was damp all over. The air was noticeably muggy and hot compared to the cool trip through the cloud.

Like jumping at night, jumping through a cloud is a unique experience, so much so that I wish everyone could experience it at least once.

WATER JUMPING

Jumping into water offers some unique advantages—and hazards. Many of us who have broken a few bones here and there in the sport have found that water jumps afford a means of continuing to jump or returning to jumping before a complete recovery.

Mari-Lou MacDonald, Canadian women's parachute champion, broke her back while skydiving, but fourteen months later she dived into the cool blue air over Toronto and drifted lazily down into her target area in the water beside the Canadian National Exhibition. It is best to wait until the casts have been removed, however, since wet casts are soon reduced to mushy plaster and long trails of gauze. Some have tried waterproofing their casts with rubber inner tubes or plastic bags, but few have been successful at it. Regardless of the physical condition of the parachutist who is making a water jump, he should observe certain basic safety rules.

Adequate flotation gear must be worn regardless of swimming ability. The military life preservers designed for pilots are excellent, since they can easily be worn under the parachute and then quickly inflated by CO_2 cartridges when needed. Shorts, T-shirt, and sneakers are adequate clothing under normal summertime conditions. Pat Catherwood, Dave Hillis, and Bill Hardman of Abbotsford, B.C., jumped into the Pacific Ocean on New Year's Day, 1970, to publicize the fiftieth annual Polar

Water jumps are fun, but have contributed to a number of parachuting fatalities in the past when proper inflation gear was not worn or when the parachutist released himself from the harness too high above the water. Here the author has stowed his reserve with instruments in a plastic bag and partially inflated his Mae West life preserver. (*Joe Rudus in* The Nashville Tennessean)

"If in doubt, whip it out!" is an old phrase in parachuting, but is still valid. Although nearly all situations now call for a jumper to cut away from a malfunction before activating the reserve, if both chutes are inflated, they will not foul each other, but rather push away from each other.

Bear Club New Year's Day swim. Although the water was reported at 42 degrees, the three survived to claim the year's first water jumps.

In an intentional water landing, it is best to avoid instruments which are difficult to keep dry. Immediately after opening, the reserve should be released to one side of the harness. When the jumper is within a hundred feet or so of the water, he should release the chest strap and grasp the inflation releases of his life jacket in each hand. Depending on the type of jacket, he may inflate one side prior to contact with the water, then inflate the other after he is in the water. If the jumper forgets to release the chest strap and inflates both sides of his life preserver, he may find himself nearly crushed as the straps restrict the inflation. Also, the chest strap may be nearly impossible to release with the intense pressure of the inflated life preserver. Quick-ejector hardware is recommended on equipment used in water jumping because it can be released with the flick of only one hand, while older V-and-snap hardware requires both hands.

A motor boat should always be used in conjunction with water jumps, and at least two persons should be aboard with extra life preservers and lines to help in an emergency.

EMERGENCY JUMP SITUATIONS

Water landings. Intentional water jumps are safe when carefully planned and properly executed, but sometimes a water jump is unintentional. This is an extremely serious situation for even the most expert of swimmers. Assuming the jumper has no flotation gear and is fully clothed for a normal landing on terra firma, he should immediately begin preparing for a water landing if there is a 50–50 chance of getting wet. He should unsnap and release the reserve to one side. Here again, quick-ejector hardware on the harness is of special advantage. If older style hardware is used, the jumper should slip the thumbs under the saddle of the harness and work it well under the buttocks so he is sitting in the saddle like a swing—no pressure on the leg straps. He should next release the leg straps, but leave the chest strap hooked until he is near the water. By now he is certain of landing on the shore or water and should have discarded helmet and gloves, and removed his boots. Giving up an expensive

Bell helmet or expensive French Paraboots is hard to do. A few have chosen to keep them on, though fewer have lived to tell of it. At about a hundred feet above the water, the jumper should release the chest strap and hang on. He should remain seated back in the saddle until contact with the water is actually made, then arch the body and slide out of the harness. He may choose to hang on to the harness if the wind is blowing toward shore. The canopy sometimes remains inflated and may act as a sail to pull him ashore, but he must be prepared to release it, if he is in danger of becoming entangled or if it is being towed away from shore. A jumpsuit or coveralls or even shirt will hold air when wet. The suit can be removed, a knot tied in the ends of each trouser leg and air forced up into the legs. This will provide emergency water wings until help arrives or until the jumper can swim ashore.

In August, 1967, eighteen jumpers bailed out of a converted WW II B-25 bomber and dropped through clouds (in direct violation of FAA regulations) to discover themselves at least one mile out over Lake Erie. Only Bernard Johnson and Robert Coy survived the tragedy, while sixteen fellow jumpers drowned. The FAA air traffic controller who had been tracking the plane on radar reported the aircraft to be six miles inland at the time of the exits. Later investigation, however, indicated some mix-up in identification of the jump plane and the photo plane which was to have photographed the jumps. Apparently the photo plane was over the field while the jump plane was over the lake, and their positions on radar had erroneously reversed. However, if the jumps had not been made over the heavy cloud cover, the jumpers would have seen that they were over water and would not have jumped.

This was one of those cases where you may get away with one small violation of safety, but the odds go up with each additional infraction. Most of the jumpers who drowned could have saved themselves by discarding equipment and inflating their jumpsuits even though they had no flotation gear, but Johnson and Coy reported a number of boats in the immediate area that were expected to help rescue the jumpers. Instead, one large cruiser moved lazily among the floundering parachutists and then turned and headed away, leaving them to drown.

If a water landing is unintentional and no flotation gear is worn, the best policy is to get rid of all excess equipment, but do not drop out of the harness until contact is made with the water. Charles Hosmer of the Air Force Academy demonstrates. (*Air Force Academy*)

By the time that many realized the boat was not coming to aid them, they had become too exhausted to discard their equipment and were dragged under. Boots, helmets, and instruments total about a hundred dollars. Parachutes could run from one to three hundred more. With a total of four hundred dollars worth of equipment, even in an emergency there is a strong resistance to throwing it all away, if there is a remote chance of saving it. In this case, the remote chance was the few boats in the area. It is far better to come back and drag for the equipment than have a rescue squad dragging for a body.

Landing in trees. Landing in trees can be fun and seldom results in injury except to the parachute. When a tree is fully clothed in leaves, it seldom damages even the parachute. This is done later by the jumper who is trying to recover it from the tree. There are two main concerns of the parachutist who is descending into a tree. First, he should avoid coming down near the center of the tree where the branches extend from the trunk and are thick, but rather aim for the springy outer branches that allow him to drop through but catch the canopy and gently pull him to a stop. Second, he should protect himself by crossing his arms in front of his face and crossing his legs so he does not straddle a branch. Since he should be wearing goggles, he should be able to keep his eyes open and see what's going on. It is possible to get turned upside down in the branches and drop through head first—a situation to be avoided, particularly if the tree is a small one that would allow the jumper to strike the ground before the canopy is caught.

Power lines. The secret to survival in the event a parachutist is being carried into power lines is to avoid touching more than one line at a time. This is one time to throw the ripcord away, if it is being carried on the wrist. (Most ripcords now remain in the ripcord housing.) The jumper should look down at the wires and keep his eyes on them so he can kick away and avoid hitting more than one wire. One unfortunate parachutist succeeded in slipping between two wires, touching only one as he went through, but the ripcord on his wrist fell across the other line. Zot! In the event the jumper lands upwind of power lines and his canopy blows over the lines, he should immediately release the canopy from the harness. It will probably continue to glide over the wires and can be retrieved on the other side. If he cannot release the canopy, he must quickly get out of the harness.

Emergency landings are serious, but not necessarily critical. The secret is to be prepared for all emergencies. Practice going through simulated emergencies so they can be quickly coped with at the proper time. The actual emergency is no time to begin practicing! Consider the thousands of lives that have been saved when a pilot made an emergency bailout with all the odds against him—and yet survived. It may be of comfort to know that many persons have survived parachute malfunctions with minor injuries. Some have survived serious injuries and returned to jump again.

After all the hairy jump stories that the newcomer is subjected to during his orientation to parachuting, he may be inclined to think his chances of survival are 50–50 at best. Actually, parachuting is as safe as any other similar sport. Safety lies in no single factor, but in a combination of factors. A parachutist must be in good physical and emotional condition to participate safely in the sport. His training and his equipment must be good.

Properly conditioned, physically and mentally, a jumper is as safe as his training and equipment. Parachutes seldom fail; it is nearly always the jumper who makes an error. A parachute is as safe as the person who uses it. Like a loaded pistol, a parachute can be a life-saver or a life-taker. A parachute must be treated with respect and care, but not with fear. Nobody can think clearly if he is filled with terror, so fear must be quickly overcome and replaced with caution. If there is still fear (not to be confused with anxiety) after a dozen or so jumps, the jumper should be encouraged to take up another sport.

Without a doubt, parachuting offers greater freedom of movement than any other sport. To be free as a bird floating weightlessly through space, is surely unique among all the active sports in the world. There is something unreal, unexplainable, about free falling through space that cannot be adequately described. Only someone who has been there can understand why sport parachuting is addictive. The obstacles to parachuting are many—money, strict governmental regulations, rigid safety standards, fear, and many hours of hard physical labor. Each jump requires time and labor in repacking the parachutes, putting on the heavy equipment and clothing, loading up and flying to jump altitude—all for a total of only a few minutes of free fall and parachute descent.

To that person who has actually done it, parachuting is the ultimate sport.

APPENDIX I
World Parachuting Championships

The First World Parachuting competition, held in Yugoslavia in 1951, was won by France. Only five nations were represented. The second world meet was held in 1954 at St. Yans, France. Army Sergeant Fred Mason was the only U.S. entrant, the first in world competition. The U.S.S.R. won the meet. In 1956, the Third World Parachuting Championships were held in Moscow and, for the first time, a U.S. team participated. Czechoslovakia placed first; the U.S., sixth. The fourth competition in Bratislava, Czechoslovakia, in 1958, was won by the U.S.S.R.

Number & Year	Place	Overall Men	Overall Women	Men's Team	Women's Team
5th 1960	Sofia, Bulgaria	Czecho-slovakia (Kaplan)		U.S.S.R.	
6th 1962	Orange, Massachu-setts	U.S.A. (Arender)	U.S.A. (Simbro)	Czecho-slovakia	U.S.A.
7th 1964	Leutkirch, West Germany	U.S.A. (Forten-berry)	U.S.A. (Taylor)	Czecho-slovakia	U.S.A.
*8th 1966	Leipzig, East Germany	U.S.S.R. (Krestjan-nikow)	U.S.S.R. (Jeremina)	U.S.S.R.	U.S.S.R.
9th 1968	Graz, Austria	U.S.S.R. (Tkats-chenko)	U.S.S.R. (Voinove)	U.S.A.	U.S.S.R.
10th 1970	Bled, Yugoslavia	U.S.S.R. (Jacmenev)	France (Baulez)	Czecho-slovakia	Czecho-slovakia

* U.S.A. did not permit a team to enter because the event was held in East Germany.

U.S. Men's Team at the 6th (1962) World Parachuting Championships. Left to right: Phil Vander Weg, Jim Arender, Dick Fortenberry, Gerry Bourquin, Hank Simbro, and Loy Brydon. This was the first World Parachuting Championship held in the United States. (*Joe Gonzales*)

U.S. Women's Team at the 6th (1962) World Parachuting Championships. Left to right: Helen Lord, Muriel Simbro, Nona Pond, Gladys Inman, and Carlyn Olson. This team won first place in overall scoring while Muriel Simbro won the Women's Individual World Champion title. (*Joe Gonzales*)

The U. S. team that competed in the 7th (1964) World Parachuting Championships at Leutkirch, West Germany. Kneeling, left to right: Maxine Hartman, Tee Taylor (who took first place as Women's World Champion), Carol Penrod, Gladys Inman, Anne Batterson (missing is Susan Clements). Standing, left to right: Team Trainer Capt. Charles Mullings, Loy Brydon, Ron Sewell, Coy McDonald, Gerry Bourquin, Bill Berg, Dick Fortenberry (who took first place as Men's World Champion), and team pilot Dave Steeves. The Women's team placed first overall while the Men's team placed third—only 3½ points behind the first-place Czechs. (*U.S. Parachuting Association*)

The 1966 U.S. National Team did not compete in the 8th World Parachuting Championships because the meet was held in East Germany. Back row, left to right: Tom Schapanski, Bobby Buscher, Bobby Letbetter (KIA, Vietnam, November, 1966), Roy Johnson, Dick Harman, Martine Durbin, Martha Huddleston, Susan Clements, Maxine Hartman. Front row, left to right: Norman Heaton, team leader; Gene Thacker, team coach. (*Joe Gonzales*)

The 1968 U.S. Team at the 9th World Championships, Graz, Austria. Back row, left to right: team photographer Chip Maury, head of delegation Charles MacCrone, team leader Lyle Cameron, Gary Lewis, Billy Lockward, Dave Sauve, Jimmy Davis, Clayton Schoelpple. Front row, left to right: FAI judge Gordon Riner, team coach Dick Harman, Karen Roach, Martha Huddleston, Susan Joerns, Barbara Roquemore, Bonnie Hickey (alternate), Annie Zurcher. (*Chip Maury*)

The 1970 U.S. Parachute Team that competed in the 10th World Parachuting Championships, Bled, Yugoslavia. Left to right: Suzie Neuman, Doug Metcalfe, Nancy Black, Bill Knight, Barbara Roquemore, Bill Hayes, Susan Rademaekers, Clayton Schoelpple, Gloria Porter, Jim Lowe, Susie Joerns, and Don Rice. (*U.S. Parachuting Association*)

APPENDIX II
Tenth World Parachuting Championships

September 6–20, 1970   Bled, Yugoslavia

RESULTS

Women Individually
Accuracy jumps from 1,000 meters

1st Zdena Zarybnicka	Czechoslovakia	0, 30
2nd Brigite Staub	France	0, 82
3rd Marie-France Baulez	France	1, 01

Style jumps from 2,000 meters

1st Valja Zakoreckaja	U.S.S.R.	27, 1,332
2nd Marie-France Baulez	France	27, 2,332
3rd Barbara Roquemore	U.S.A.	27, 6,333

Overall

1st Marie-France Baulez	France	4, 7,914
2nd Valja Zakoreckaja	U.S.S.R.	5, 0,447
3rd Carol Brand	Canada	5, 2,889

Women's team
Group accuracy jumps from 1,000 meters

1st France	6, 44
2nd U.S.S.R.	7, 58
3rd Bulgaria	8, 87

Overall

1st Czechoslovakia	25, 7,486
2nd U.S.S.R.	25, 9,356
3rd Bulgaria	28, 7,210

Men individually
Accuracy jumps from 1,000 meters

1st Donald E. Rice	U.S.A.	0, 12
2nd Vjaceslav Sarabanov	U.S.S.R.	0, 14
3rd Milan Dimic	Yugoslavia	0, 22

Style jumps from 2,000 meters

1st Aleksej Jacmenev	U.S.S.R.	22, 2,666
2nd Josef Pospichal	Czechoslovakia	22, 4,999
3rd Vladimir Gurnij	U.S.S.R.	22, 9,999

Overall

1st Aleksej Jacmenev	U.S.S.R.	4, 0,136
2nd Joseph Pospichal	Czechoslovakia	4, 1,975
3rd Vjaceslav Sarabanov	U.S.S.R.	4, 2,794

Men's team
  Group accuracy jumps from 1,000 meters
    1st Czechoslovakia   1, 10
    2nd Yugoslavia   2, 45
    3rd Canada   3, 64

  Overall
    1st Czechoslovakia   18, 2,353
    2nd U.S.S.R.   20, 9,816
    3rd Canada   22, 1,180

OFFICIAL RULES

FOR THE 10TH WORLD PARACHUTING CHAMPIONSHIPS

N. B.   No departure from these Rules is permitted. Each participant and each national Aero Club participating in the Championships either with a team or an individual competitor accepts the conditions set out in the text below of the Official Rules.

I.   AIMS OF THE 10TH WORLD CHAMPIONSHIPS

1.1.   To determine the following World Parachute Champions—men and women separately:
World Parachute Champion in precision jumps
World Parachute Champion in style jumps
Absolute World Parachute Champion
World Parachute Champion in group precision jumps
World Parachute Champion by team

1.2.   To establish new world records.

1.3.   To popularise and improve parachuting as a sport.

1.4.   To facilitate the exchange of experience acquired in sport parachuting.

1.5.   To strengthen friendly relations between sportsmen of participating countries.

II.   DATE AND PLACE OF THE 10TH WORLD CHAMPIONSHIPS

2.1.   The 10th World Championships will be held from September 4th to September 21st, 1970, at Bled (Yugoslavia) at the sport airport Lesce-Bled.

III. GENERAL RULES

3.1. Only persons or teams who are members of national Aero Clubs affiliated or associated with the F.A.I. may take part in the 10th World Championships.

3.2. The World Championships for men and women will be held provided at least 6 men's and 6 women's national teams are present. If less than 6 men's teams but 6 or more women's teams are present, the Championships will be for women only. If 6 or more men's national teams and less than 6 women's teams are present, the Championships will be for men only.

IV. ORGANIZATION AND CONDUCT OF THE 10TH WORLD CHAMPIONSHIPS

4.1. The Aeronautical Union of Yugoslavia has been authorized by F.A.I. to organize and conduct the 10th World Championships.

V. ACCOMMODATION AND FOOD FOR PARTICIPANTS

5.1. Accommodation and food shall be provided by the Organizer.

VI. TRANSPORT

6.1. Local transport during the time of the Championships shall be provided by the Organizer.

6.2. Travelling expenses to and from the place of the 10th World Championships shall be met by the competitors themselves.

VII. COMPOSITION OF DELEGATIONS

7.1. Each delegation may be composed of the following maximum number of persons:
the Head of the Delegation (if possible, a national representative on the C.I.P. of the F.A.I.)
an International Judge
the Team Leader
a Pilot
an Interpreter
a Doctor
Men's Team, consisting of 5 men's competitors
Women's Team, consisting of 5 women's competitors

7.2. Each men's team or women's team shall be set up of at least 4 competitors. If the number of competitors is smaller than 4 the participating country may compete only in the individual events.

7.3. The competitors may compete in all events or only in some events.

7.4. Each team participating in group jumps shall be composed of four competitors.

VIII. CONDITIONS OF PARTICIPATION

8.1. Entries:

Entries for the 10th World Championships shall be sent through the participant's national Acro Club to reach the Organizers by July 5th, 1970 to the following address:

Organizacijski komite X. SPP
Ljubljana
Lepi pot 6—PP 496
Jugoslavija

8.2. Changes in the teams shall be permissible until the beginning of the Championships.

8.3. Entrance fee:

Each member of a participating delegation shall pay an entrance fee in the amount of U.S. $119.00

8.4. The above amount shall be sent at the same time as the entry form to the following address:

Zveza letalskih organizacij Slovenije
X. svetovno padalsko prvenstvo
KB 501-620-7-32002-10-276 Ljubljana

IX. SPORTING LICENSES AND MEDICAL CERTIFICATES

9.1 Before the beginning of the Championships, Team Leaders shall produce for their competitors Sporting Licenses (according to the Sporting Code, Part I, Section 2, Item 2.1.1) issued by the national Aero Club as well as Medical Certificates of fitness for parachute jumping with information of the blood group and rhesus factor.

9.2. The pilot of a team must hold a sporting pilot's license valid for the current year, issued by the competent organization of his country.

9.3. The minimum age for each competitor is 18 years.

X. EQUIPMENT FOR WHICH THE PARTICIPANTS ARE RESPONSIBLE

10.1 Each competitor shall equip himself with the following:
main parachute
a safety parachute
a protective helmet

10.2. As regards the rest of the equipment and clothing: gloves, combination suit, etc., the rules of the Sporting Code, Part V, D 2-a shall apply.

10.3. The parachutes may be of any type provided they have been approved by the National competent authorities.

10.4. The maximum speed of a parachute when tested with a weight of 100 Kgs must be 6.5 seconds. This speed must be certified.

10.5. This certificate must be produced by the Team Leader to the Organizer.

XI. AIRCRAFT AND EQUIPMENT FOR WHICH THE ORGANIZER IS RESPONSIBLE

11.1. For jumping purposes aircrafts of AN-2 type will be available. These aircrafts have dual controls so that each team can be piloted by its own pilot.

11.2. The second pilot shall be provided by the Organizer but he shall not act as a pilot for the team of his own country.

11.3. The jumping height shall be controlled by a barograph and an altimeter which shall be visible both to the judge and to the competitors.

11.4. A sufficient number of canvases shall be available.

XII. METEOROLOGICAL CONDITIONS

12.1. Competition in jumps for precision of landing will be held provided the wind speed at ground level does not exceed 7 m/sec for men and 6 m/sec for women; and competition in style jumps will be held provided the wind speed at ground level does not exceed 8 m/sec for men and 7 m/sec for women.

12.2. The ground-level wind situation shall be indicated by a recording anemometer, a windsock, and special panels. The meteorological situation shall be announced 30 minutes before the start of the competition, and current meteorological situation every thirty minutes throughout the competition. Before the beginning of the competition a test jump shall be made, but in case of danger a paper wind drift indicator shall be dropped.

12.3. If after a decision has been made to stop jumps, one or more parachutists land, their jumps may be recommenced.

12.4. Questions arising from requests to recommence a jump because of dubious wind conditions shall be settled by the Committee of Judges.

XIII. EVENTS AND MARKING OF PERFORMANCES

13.1. Event No. 1:
Individual precision jumps from an altitude of 1.000 metres with delayed opening of parachute from 0 to 10 seconds.

Each competitor shall make four jumps; all the jumps shall be marked. Points shall be given for precision of landing only.

If, after the four jumps, more than one competitor has achieved the best score these competitors shall make another three jumps each. The three jumps shall be marked according to the conditions stated above and shall be considered only for the purpose of determining the World Champion in precision jumps.

When determining the Absolute World Parachute Champion and the Team World Parachute Champion the first four jumps only shall be considered.

13.2. Event No. 2:

Individual style jumps from an altitude of 2.000 metres with maximum delayed opening of parachute of 30 seconds.

If meteorological conditions do not allow jumps from an altitude of 2.000 metres, the altitude may be lowered to 1.800 metres with maximum delayed opening of 25 seconds.

Each competitor shall make three jumps; all the jumps shall be marked. During the time of free descent each competitor shall carry out the following series of figures:

In the 1st jump:	In the 2nd jump:	In the 3rd jump:
left spiral	right spiral	left spiral
right spiral	left spiral	right spiral
backloop	backloop	backloop
left spiral	right spiral	right spiral
right spiral	left spiral	left spiral
backloop	backloop	backloop

When jumping, competitors leave the aircraft when it is situated between the two orange coloured strips placed on the ground in the direction of the arrow. One of the strips is placed 1.300 metres and the other 800 metres from the arrow.

13.3. Event No. 3:

Group precision jumps from an altitude of 1.000 metres with delayed opening of the parachute from 0 to 10 seconds.

Each team shall make three jumps;

All the jumps shall be marked;

Points shall be given for precision of landing only.

13.4. The marking of the results shall be done according to the U.S. scoring system, which is appended to the Official Rules.

XIV. CONDITIONS FOR THE EXECUTION OF JUMPS

14.1. The Landing Area:

The Landing Area shall be traced by a circle 100 metres in radius. In the middle of this circle there shall be prepared a pit, covered with sand, with a radius of 25 metres, in the centre of which there shall be a circular disc 10 centimetres in diameter. At a distance of 5 metres from the centre there shall be placed a cross of orange colour and of the dimensions 5 x 1 metre.

14.2. Permission for, and prohibition of, jumping:
Jumping is permitted if all arms of the cross are fully laid out. If one arm is folded, jumping is permitted for men only. If all the four arms are folded, jumping is prohibited. All the aircrafts should land.

14.3. For all the jumps the competitor shall be allowed one passage of the aircraft only. If, after this passage he desires a second passage, he must request the approval of the judge on board the aircraft. Approval shall not be unduly refused. If he does not jump at the second passage, he shall not be allowed another one.

14.4. The direction of the flight and the point at which the competitor leaves the aircraft are the choice of the competitor, except in style event when the direction of flight and the jumping point are selected over an area chosen by the Organizer in agreement with the Chief Judge.

14.5. Order of jumping:
a. Precision jumps
The order of the jumping of teams shall be determined by ballot. The order of jumping of competitors inside a team shall be fixed by the Team Leader.
b. Style jumps
The order of boarding the aircraft shall be settled by ballot and the jumps shall be made in an order determined by a ballot held by the judge on board the aircraft after take-off.

14.6. If in emergency a parachutist has used his reserve parachute the Committee of Judges may authorize a second jump, except in the case of style events.

14.7. No ground signals visible to the parachutists and no instructions in sound are permitted. If use is made of such signals or instructions the jump shall be disallowed.

14.8. Medical help
During the competition a Doctor shall be at disposal. A competitor who has fallen ill or has suffered injury may, after consulting the Doctor and with the agreement of his Team Leader, continue jumping. The competitor may make the jumps he has missed unless the particular event has been finished.

XV. THE COMMITTEE OF TEAM LEADERS

15.1. The Team Leaders of the participating countries represent an international commission which shall lend its assistance to the Organizer where questions of organization which affect the teams (such as changes of programme, etc.) are concerned. The right to vote is confined to those Team Leaders who represent either a complete masculine or a complete feminine team. In no. case shall this Committee function as International Jury.

XVI. THE PANEL OF INTERNATIONAL JUDGES

16.1. Assessment of performances shall be marked by the Panel of Judges selected from the official F.A.I. list of Judges.

16.2. International Judges must so far as possible be in possession of International Certificate F and must obligatorily possess, at least, Certificate D with a valid license.

16.3. On the proposal of the Organizer, C.I.P. designated for Chief-Judge— Mr. Daryl HENRY (Canada), and for Assistant to the Chief-Judge— Mr. Janko LUTOVAC (Yugoslavia).

16.4. The International Parachuting Committee has asked the national Aero Clubs of the following countries to send a Judge:
Austria
Bulgaria
Czechoslovakia
East Germany
France
Italy
Poland
Soviet Union
Switzerland
United States
West Germany
and for reserves:
Hungary
Ireland
Rumania
Spain
Sweden

XVII. DETERMINATION OF WORLD CHAMPIONS

17.1. World Parachute Champion in precision jumps (men and women separately):
The title of World Parachute Champion in precision jumps shall be awarded to the competitor who has gained the best score in event No. 1.

17.2. World Parachute Champion in style jumps (men and women separately):
The title of World Parachute Champion in style jumps shall be awarded to the competitor who has gained the best score in event No. 2.

17.3. Absolute World Parachute Champion—in combination of precision jumps and style jumps—(men and women separately):

The title of Absolute World Parachute Champion shall be awarded to the competitor who has gained the best score determined on the basis of adding the number of points for precision jumps (only the first 4 jumps are considered)

and ½ (one-half) of the points for style jumps.

17.4. Team World Parachute Champion (men and women separately):

The title of the Team World Parachute Champion shall be awarded to the team that has gained the best score in event No. 3.

17.5. Absolute Team World Parachute Champion (men and women separately):

The title of the Absolute Team World Parachute Champion shall be awarded to the team that has gained the best score

a. of the four best men, and the four best women respectively, in event No. 1 and No. 2, together with

b. all the points earned by the team in event No. 3.

17.6. In case an equal number of points has been earned by more than one competitor (or more than one team), their status shall be considered to be ex aequo.

XVIII. INTERNATIONAL JURY

18.1. The International Jury shall be composed of at least three members of the F.A.I. International Parachuting Committee who shall be attending the competition.

18.2. The International Jury is responsible for seeing that the provisions of the Sporting Code and of these Official Rules are observed.

18.3. The International Jury, on the basis of Sporting Code, shall deal with all the objections and protests which the Panel of Judges has not managed to settle. Only members of the Jury who are permanent members of the F.A.I. CIP shall take part in the votes.

XIX. OBJECTIONS AND PROTESTS

19.1. Each protest or objection must be submitted in writing, according to the Part V, Section I of the Sporting Code.

19.2. Each competitor taking part in the Championships and each national Aero Club agrees thereby to accept all the decisions of the International Jury as final.

XX. SUPPLEMENTARY PROVISIONS

20.1. To settle questions not covered by the present Official Rules the F.A.I. Sporting Code shall be used as basis.

20.2. In case of diverging interpretations of the present Official Rules the French text of the same Rules shall be regarded as officially valid.

Sporting Commission of
the Aeronautical Union
of Yugoslavia

SCORING SYSTEM

Event No. 1

1. The precision of landing shall be measured at a distance not exceeding 10,00 metres.

2. Landing in the centre brings the competitor 0,00; for each 1 metre from the rim of the disk in the centre the competitor is given 1.00, which is in other terms for each 1 centimetre 0,01.

3. Landing at a distance of 10 metres from the rim of the disk in the centre brings 10.00; any landing outside the distance of 10.00 metres from the centre likewise brings 10.00.

4. The result in this event shall be determined by summing the results achieved in individual jumps which sum shall be divided by the number of jumps (arithmetical average).

5. The winner in the event is the competitor who has achieved the lowest number of points.

6. In case the competitor opens the parachute after the 10 seconds from the time of the jump-offs, he is given a penalty of 2.00.

Event No. 2

1. In this event the time of performing the series of figures within 16 seconds shall be scored. Each second brings the competitor 1.00, which is in other terms for each 0.1 second 0.1. If the series of figures is performed in a period of time exceeding 16 seconds, the competitor is given 16.00.

2. The competitor can start with his series of figures at any time according to his discretion when 5 seconds from the time of his leaving the aircraft have passed.

3. The judge shall start the chronometre when in the position of the competitor he notices a visible change as regards the course of the flight of the aircraft or as regards the direction of the arrow.

4. The judge shall stop the chronometre when the competitor has finished his last loop and remained in a horizontal position with his head in the direction of the arrow for at least 1 second.

5. The points for style jumps come from the time of performing the figures and from the penalty points.

6. The penalty points are as follows:

a. Undershoots	0–25 degrees	0,5 seconds
	26–45 degrees	1,0 seconds
	46–90 degrees	3,5 seconds
	greater than 90 degrees	16,0 seconds
b. Overshoots	0–45 degrees	0 seconds
	46–90 degrees	0 seconds
	91–180 degrees	1,0 seconds
	181–270 degrees	3,5 seconds
	greater than 270 degrees	16,0 seconds
c. Last backloop off heading	0–25 degrees	0 seconds
	26–45 degrees	1,0 seconds
	46–90 degrees	3,5 seconds
	greater than 90 degrees	16,0 seconds

d. Execution of a turn or backloop with the body tilted or banked in excess of 45 degrees

pitch greater than 45 degrees	1,0 seconds
roll greater than 45 degrees	0,5 seconds

e. Omission of manoeuvre, added manoeuvre or incorrect series .... 16,0 seconds

7. The result in this event shall be determined by summing the results achieved in individual jumps which sum shall be divided by the number of jumps (arithmetical average), and this result shall be further divided by 2.

8. The winner in the event is the competitor who has achieved the lowest number of points.

9. In case the competitor opens his parachute after 30 seconds from the time of leaving the aircraft, he shall be given a penalty of 3.5 seconds when jumping the altitude of 2,000 metres, or after 25 seconds when jumping from an altitude of 1,800 metres.

Event No. 3

1. The scoring of the results shall be done in the same way as explained for event No. 1.

2. The result in this event is determined by summing the average result of the jumps of the individual competitors in the group.

3. The winner in the event is the group which has achieved the lowest number of points.

4. In case the first competitor in the group opens his parachute after 10 seconds from the time of the jump-off, the group is given a penalty of 2.00.

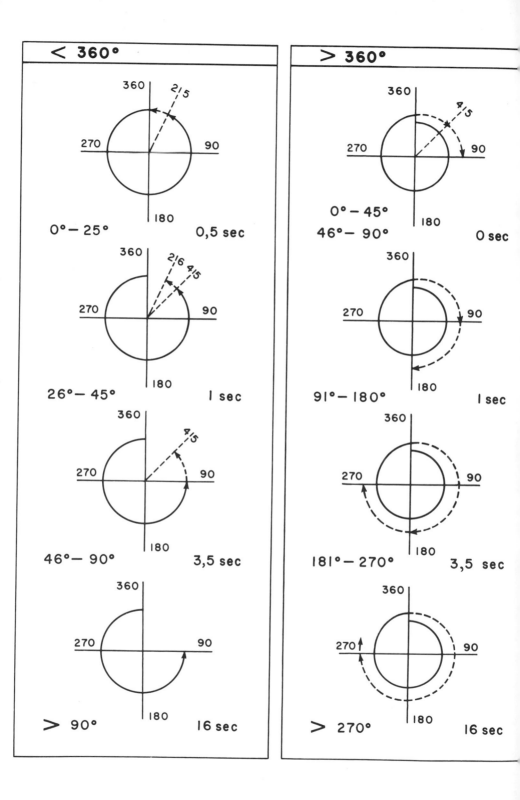

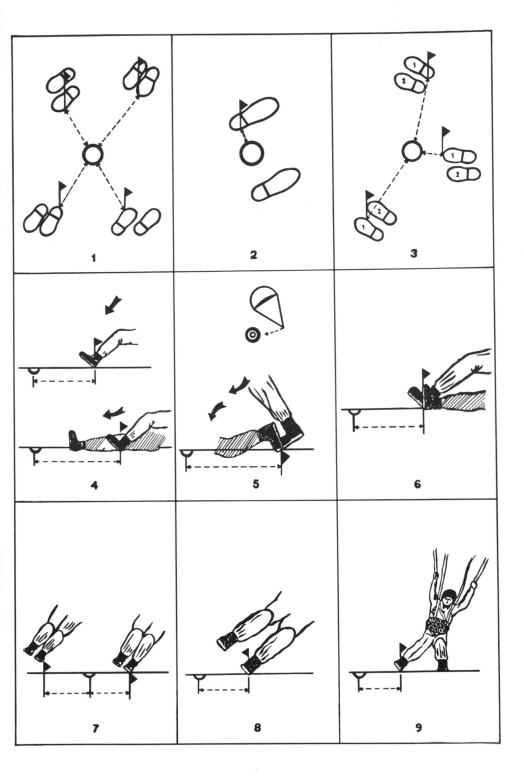

1

2

3

4

5

6

7

8

9

APPENDIX III

USPA* Basic Safety Regulations

SUBPART A—GENERAL

100:01 APPLICABILITY
(a) This Part prescribes rules governing all parachute jumps made in the United States, except:

1. Parachute jumps necessary because of an in-flight emergency; and

2. Parachute jumps made while under Military orders to perform such jumps when these orders require that the parachute jump be of a nature contrary to these regulations.

(b) For the purpose of this Part, a "parachute jump" means the descent of a person to the surface from an aircraft in flight when he intends to use, or uses a parachute during all or part of that descent.

(c) All persons participating in parachuting should be familiar with:

1. Part 10, USPA Publications (Definitions);
2. Part 100, USPA Publications (these regulations);
3. Part 101, USPA Publications (Waivers to the BSRs);
4. Part 104, USPA Publications (USPA Licenses);
5. USPA Doctrine; and
6. All Federal, State and local regulations and rules pertaining to parachuting.

100.11 COMPLIANCE WITH REGULATIONS

No parachute jump shall be made in violation of Federal Aviation Administration regulations.

SUBPART B—ADMINISTRATIVE

100.13 MEDICAL REQUIREMENTS

All persons engaging in parachuting shall:
(a) Carry a valid Class I, II or III Federal Aviation Administration Medical Certificate; or
(b) Carry a certificate of physical fitness for parachuting from a registered physician; or
(c) Have completed the USPA Medical Certificate.

100.15 AGE REQUIREMENTS

Civilian parachutists shall be at least:
(a) 21 years of age; or
(b) 16 years of age with notarized parental or guardian consent.

* United States Parachute Association Publications.

SUBPART C—OPERATIONS

100.21 NOVICE PARACHUTISTS

(a) All novice parachute jumps must be made under the *direct* supervision of a currently rated USPA Jumpmaster aboard the aircraft until the novice has been certified by his CSO, ASO, USPA Instructor or USPA Instructor/Examiner to jumpmaster himself.

(b) Novice parachutists must:

1. Initially make five (5) static line sport parachute jumps;
2. Successfully pull a dummy ripcord prior to canopy inflation on three (3) successive static line jumps without loss of stability or control.

(c) Maximum ground winds for novice parachutists: 10 m.p.h.

100.23 MINIMUM OPENING ALTITUDES

Minimum pack opening altitudes above the ground for parachutists shall be:

(a) Student and Novice parachutists: 2,500 ft. above the ground.
(b) Class A and B License holders: 2,500 ft. above the ground.
(c) Class C License holders: 2,000 ft. above the ground.
(d) Class D License holders: 2,000 ft. above the ground.

100.25 DROP ZONE REQUIREMENTS

(a) All areas used for parachuting must be unobstructed, with the following minimum radial distances to the nearest hazard:

1. Student and Novice parachutists: 300 meters.
2. Class A and B License holders: 200 meters.
3. Class C License holders: 100 meters.
4. Class D License holders: Unlimited.

NOTE: Hazards are defined as: trees, ditches, telephone and power lines, towers, buildings, highways, and automobiles.

(b) Manned ground-to-air communications (e.g., radios, panels, smoke, lights) must be present on the drop zone during parachuting operations.

100.27 PRE-JUMP REQUIREMENTS

The appropriate altitude and surface winds will be determined prior to conducting any parachute jump.

100.29 EXTRAORDINARY PARACHUTE JUMPS

(a) Night, water, and exhibition parachute jumps may be performed with the approval of the local USPA Area Safety Officer (ASO) or USPA Instructor/Examiner.

(b) Pre-planned breakaway jumps may be made only by Class C and Class D License holders using FAA TSO'ed equipment.

(c) Batwings are prohibited. ("Batwings" are defined as any jumpsuit extensions that extend past the elbow or extend past the waist or below the knees or have any rigid or semi-rigid parts· or any other device that may restrict the arm or leg movements of the jumper in freefall.)

SUBPART D—EQUIPMENT

100.31 PARACHUTISTS EQUIPMENT

Each parachutist must be equipped with:
(a) A rigid or semi-rigid helmet;
(b) Flotation gear when the intended exit point, opening point or landing point of a parachutist is within one mile of a open body of water (an open body of water is defined as one in which a parachutist could drown); and
(c) A flashing light when performing night jumps.

100.41 SPECIAL ALTITUDE EQUIPMENT, SUPPLEMENTARY OXYGEN

Supplementary oxygen is mandatory on parachute jumps performed over 15,000 feet (MSL).

PART 104—USPA LICENSES AND CERTIFICATES

INTRODUCTION

The United States Parachute Association is authorized by the National Aeronautic Association and the Federal Aeronautique Internationale to issue parachuting licenses in the general interest of sporting aviation. Parachuting licenses and certificates are issued by the USPA on the basis of ability, proficency and knowledge and are spaced at different levels to represent significant degrees of experience.

SUBPART A—ADMINISTRATION

104.01 GENERAL

This Part specifies the procedures and requirements for:
a. Qualifications for certificates and FAI parachuting licenses issued by the USPA;
b. Issuance of foreign aero club FAI licenses to United States citizens;
c. Issuance of USPA licenses to foreign nationals; and
d. License renewal.

104.02 ADMINISTRATIVE PROCEDURES

a. Sporting licenses issued by the USPA will be valid for not more than one calendar year and will remain valid through the 31st of December of the year.
b. The sporting license shall be valid in all countries represented in the FAI, and, during the validity of the license, shall entitle the holder to participate in any open sport parachuting event organized in any of these countries (**FAI Sporting Code,** Section 1, paragraph 4.2.4).
c. Parachuting licenses and certificates issued by the USPA may be issued to USPA members who satisfy the conditions as set forth for the particular license.
d. "Military Parachute Jumps" (refer to USPA Part 10) made during service with the armed forces and officially recorded may be used to satisfy requirements for obtaining all classes of licenses, except that an initial license

application from any person trained via "military parachute jumps" who has not made sport type static line jumps such as are required for the Class A License in the USPA Basic Safety Regulations, must be accompanied by certification from an ASO, a USPA Instructor/Examiner, or USPA Instructor that the applicant is capable of making controlled freefalls and remaining stable during manual deployment of the parachute in terminal freefall.

e. Parachute jumps offered as evidence of parachuting must:

1. Have been made in accordance with the requirements and regulations of the USPA in existence at the time of the jump.

2. Be legibly recorded and certified in chronological order in an appropriate log that contains the following minimum information: date, location of jump, type of jump, aircraft type, duration of delayed freefall in seconds (if applicable), landing distance from a target (if used), wind conditions, type of equipment used, and freefall maneuvers (as applicable).

3. Have been made with **manual activation** the intended method for parachute deployment. (Automatic devices must be used only as a back-up for failure to deploy the parachute manually.)

f. **Certification:** Parachute jumps for number must be certified by an FAI-licensed parachutist who personally witnessed the jump or the pilot of the jump aircraft (to include name, type of license, and license number). Parachute jumps for performance (e.g., figure eight, etc.) may be certifed **only** by a licensed parachutist who witnessed the jump. FAI licenses need not be current to validate certification.

g. The license application form must, prior to submission to USPA Headquarters, be certified correct by a USPA Instructor/Examiner or the ASO for the applicant's area; or, in the case of a Class A License, by the applicant's CSO or the USPA Instructor who is responsible for the training given the applicant/novice.

h. Where freefall jumps of specified delays are required, jumps of longer delays automatically cover time requirements for lesser delays.

i. Proficiency requirements for licenses, such as demonstrations of ability or knowledge, must be certified by the applicant's CSO, ASO, a USPA Instructor, or USPA Instructor/Examiner who holds an equal or higher license.

j. **First Jump and First Freefall** certificates may be certified only by a CSO, ASO, USPA Instructor, or USPA Instructor/Examiner.

k. Applicants for licenses and ratings are responsible for forwarding required forms, fees, and photographs to USPA Headquarters. Applicants for Class D licenses will include the logbooks containing the qualifying jumps with the license application.

l. Licenses may be renewed by remitting to USPA Headquarters the appropriate renewal fees and by showing proof of current qualification. Such qualification must be certified by the applicant's CSO, ASO, a USPA Instructor, or USPA Instructor/Examiner.

m. USPA Directors are empowered to certify Instructor/Examiner applications, annual license validations, and Gold Wing qualifications whether or not they hold the license or rating otherwise required.

n. USPA/FAI licenses may not be refused, suspended, or revoked unless such action is authorized by the Board of Directors of the USPA or unless such action is in accord with existing administrative directives.

o. For the purpose of this Part the term "controlled" refers to the parachutist having effective control over the position of his body.

104.03 ISSUANCE OF USPA LICENSES TO FOREIGN NATIONALS

a. Foreign nationals desiring any USPA license must meet all requirements of Part 104 for the license desired.

b. Citizens of foreign countries which have a National Aero Club recognized by the FAI must show proof that permission has been granted by their NAC for the USPA license desired.

c. Citizens of foreign countries which do not have a National Aero Club recognized by the FAI or persons without nationality may be issued USPA licenses provided they meet all other requirements.

104.04 ISSUANCE OF FOREIGN LICENSES TO U.S. CITIZENS

Applicant must:

a. Meet the requirements of that foreign Aero Club.

b. Possess a currently valid USPA license of equivalent letter designation (e.g., an applicant for a foreign Class D license must already possess a valid USPA Class D License).

SUBPART B—CERTIFICATES AND LICENSES

104.05 USPA FIRST JUMP CERTIFICATE

The individual must:

a. Have successfully completed all training required;

b. Have made his first sport static line parachute jump.

104.06 USPA FREEFALL CERTIFICATE

The Novice must:

a. Have qualified for the USPA First Jump Certificate;

b. Have successfully completed at least five sport static line parachute jumps; and

c. Have successfully completed one freefall parachute jump with a manual deployment of the parachute.

104.07 CLASS A LICENSE—PARACHUTIST

Persons who hold a Class A License are certified as able to jumpmaster themselves, pack their own main parachute, and compete in USPA competitions. The applicant must have:

a. Completed 25 freefall parachute jumps (refer to USPA PART 111.08, Progression) including:

1. 12 controlled delays of at least 10 seconds.

2. 6 controlled delays of at least 20 seconds.

3. 3 controlled delays of at least 30 seconds.

4. 10 freefall jumps landing within 50 meters of target center during which the novice selected the exit and opening points.

b. Demonstrated ability to hold heading during freefall and make 360 degree flat turns to both the right and left.

c. Demonstrated ability to safely jumpmaster himself, to include independently selecting the proper altitude and properly using correct exit and opening points.

d. Demonstrated ability to properly pack his own main parachute and conduct safety checks on his and other parachutist's equipment prior to a jump.

e. A logbook endorsement by a USPA Instructor/Examiner, a USPA Instructor, his CSO or ASO that he had received training for unintentional water landings.

f. Passed a written examination conducted by his CSO, ASO, USPA Instructor, or USPA Instructor/Examiner.

License Fee: $5.00.

104.08 CLASS B LICENSE—INTERMEDIATE

Persons who hold a Class B License are certified as able to jumpmaster themselves, pack their own main parachute, are eligible for appointment as Club Safety Officer, and are recognized as having reached the level of proficiency to safely perform relative work and to participate in competition and record attempts. The applicant must have:

a. Met all requirements for the Class A license.

b. Completed 50 controlled freefall parachute jumps (refer to USPA PART 111.08, Progression) including:

1. 15 delays of at least 30 seconds;

2. 2 delays of at least 45 seconds.

c. Demonstrated his ability to complete two alternate 360 degree flat turns to the right and left (Figure 8) followed by a backloop in freefall in ten seconds or less.

d. Landed within 25 meters of target center on 10 jumps during which he selected the exit and opening points.

e. Demonstrated his ability to control and vary both his rate of descent and lateral movement.

f. Demonstrated his ability to move to a horizontal distance from another jumper such that they could safely pull at the same time. Demonstrate that he knows how to and has adequate control in freefall to be able to thoroughly check the sky around himself before pulling. (This demonstration of horizontal separation and looking before pulling must be done in 7 seconds or less. It will be verified by an experienced relative worker.) Demonstrate his ability to keep track of other canopies and remain a safe distance from them.

g. Passed a written examination conducted by a USPA Instructor/Examiner, USPA Instructor, his CSO, or ASO.

License Fee: $10.00.

104.09 CLASS C LICENSE—ADVANCED

Persons who hold a Class C License are certified as able to jumpmaster licensed parachutists, pack their own main parachute; are eligible for appointment as Club Safety Officer and Area Safety Officer; are recognized as having reached the proficiency level to participate in competition; make relative work, night, water, and exhibition jumps; participate in record attempts; and are eligible for the Jumpmaster and Instructor Ratings. The applicant must have:

a. Met all requirements for the Class B License.

b. Completed 100 controlled freefall parachute jumps including:

1. 30 controlled delays of at least 30 seconds;

2. 5 controlled delays of at least 45 seconds.

c. Demonstrated his ability to perform a controlled international series (Figure 8, Back Loop, Figure 8, Back Loop) in freefall in less than 18 seconds.

d. Landed within 15 meters of target center on 25 freefall jumps during which the parachutist independently selected the exit point.

e. Demonstrate ability to "track."

f. Demonstrated the ability to control and coordinate rate of descent and horizontal movement by exiting the aircraft as high man and, by acting as aggressor, moving to and in a smooth coordinated manner making contact with an experienced relative worker acting as base.

g. Passed a written examination conducted by a USPA Instructor/Examiner, USPA Instructor, his CSO, or ASO.

License Fee: $15.00.

104.10 CLASS D LICENSE—EXPERT

Persons who hold a Class D License are certified as able to jumpmaster licensed parachutists, pack their own main parachute; may compete; participate in record attempts; make relative work, night, water, and exhibition jumps; are eligible for USPA Jumpmaster, Instructor, and Instructor/Examiner Ratings; and are eligible for appointment as Club Safety Officer or Area Safety Officer. The applicant must have:

a. Met all requirements for the Class C License.

b. Completed 200 controlled freefall parachute jumps including:

1. 100 delays of at least 20 seconds;

2. 40 delays of at least 30 seconds;

3. 5 delays of at least 45 seconds;

4. 5 delays of at least 60 seconds.

c. Demonstrated his ability to perform the following maneuvers on heading in 18 seconds or less: Back Loop, Front Loop, Left Turn, Right Turn, Right Barrel Roll, Left Barrel Roll.

d. Landed within 2 meters of target center on 10 freefall delays during which the parachutist independently selected the exit and opening points.

e. Made one night parachute jump with a delay of at least 20 seconds, with certification of prior night jump training (USPA Instructor/Examiner, USPA Instructor, his CSO, or ASO). Jump must be approved by ASO in accordance with USPA BSRs.

f. Make one intentional water jump with certification of prior intentional water jump training (USPA Instructor/Examiner, USPA Instructor, his CSO, or ASO). Jump must be approved by ASO in accordance with USPA BSRs.

g. Passed a written examination conducted by a USPA Instructor/Examiner, USPA Instructor, or his ASO.

License Fee: $20.00.

SUBPART C—ANNUAL VALIDATION REQUIREMENTS

104.21 CLASS A LICENSE

a. Must be a member of the USPA; and
b. Must have completed 5 controlled delays during the preceding 12 month period.

104.22 CLASS B LICENSE

a. Must be a member of the USPA; and
b. Must have completed 5 controlled delays during the preceding 12 month period.

104.23 CLASS C LICENSE

a. Must be a member of the USPA; and
b. Must have completed 5 controlled delays during the preceding 12 month period.

104.24 CLASS D LICENSE

a. Must be a member of the USPA; and
b. Must have completed 10 controlled delays during the preceding 12 month period.

APPENDIX IV
Gold Expert Parachute Badge with Diamonds

Awarded to those USPA members holding the US/FAI Class D License who have recorded 12 hours of free-fall time, all jumps being made under the provisions of the Basic Safety Regulations. It must be verified by a Conference or National Director, or by USPA Headquarters.

Paul Poppenhager	Florida	
Leo Kryske	North Carolina	10 Sep 1968
Gene Thacker	North Carolina	10 Sep 1968
Roy Johnson	Ohio	6 Jul 1968
Jim West	Ohio	21 Apr 1969
Billy Lockward	Arizona	10 Sep 1968
Eric Bahor	Ohio	5 Dec 1968
Jimmy Godwin	Florida	13 Dec 1968
Jim Stoyas	Illinois	13 Dec 1968
Jimmy L. Davis	North Carolina	26 Dec 1968
Raymond Duffy	North Carolina	18 Feb 1969
Ted Mayfield	Oregon	4 Jul 1969
Woody Binnicker	South Carolina	15 Sep 1969
Davis C. Sims	Georgia	15 Sep 1969
Donald F. Strickland	APO, NYC	1 Oct 1969
David A. Espen	Arizona	26 Dec 1969
David Sauve	Michigan	12 Jan 1970
Hector Nunez	California	18 Jan 1970
William C. Hayes	Missouri	22 Jun 1970
Sherman K. Hawkins	North Carolina	22 Jun 1970
Jim Lowe	Oregon	8 Jul 1970
Tom Schapanski	Illinois	30 Sep 1970
Michael J. Howard	North Carolina	30 Sep 1970
Earl J. Cossey	Washington	22 Oct 1970
George W. Edwards	California	6 Nov 1970

Index